111 Most Common Regrets of the Dying That You Can Avoid Today

111 Most Common Regrets of the Dying That You Can Avoid Today

A Life Without Regrets to Make Wiser Choices, Find Purpose, and Live with Fulfillment Before It's Too Late

Aria Capri Publishing Group

Mauricio Vasquez

Toronto, Canada

Authors:
Aria Capri Publishing Group
Mauricio Vasquez

First Printing: March 2025

ISBN 978-1-998729-12-8 (Electronic book)
ISBN 978-1-998729-11-1 (Hardcover book)
ISBN 978-1-998729-10-4 (Paperback)

Living Without Regrets: A Personal Journey

Have you ever found yourself lying awake at night, replaying moments you wish you'd handled differently? Those quiet, vulnerable hours when memories flood in, and you wonder about the paths not taken? I know I have. My journey through life has become a careful dance of intention—a constant effort to live in a way that won't leave me with a heart full of "what ifs" when I look back.

Every day feels like a collection of small crossroads. Should I call my parents or send another text? Take that career risk or play it safe? Speak up or stay silent? These aren't just decisions; they're the brushstrokes that will ultimately paint the entire canvas of my life. I've realized that time doesn't just pass—it flows, carrying our choices like leaves on a river, each one shaping the journey ahead.

There's a profound difference between existing and truly living. I've watched too many people around me drift through life on autopilot, only to wake up years later wondering where their dreams went. I refuse to be one of those people. My goal isn't perfection, but authenticity. It's about making conscious choices that resonate with my deepest values, even when—especially when—those choices are challenging.

This book isn't a lecture or a list of rules. It's a companion for anyone who's ever felt the weight of unexplored potential. By sharing stories of regret—not to discourage, but to illuminate—I hope to offer a mirror. A chance for each reader to pause, reflect, and realize that we're not alone in our fears, our hesitations, our hopes.

We all have the power to rewrite our story, one choice at a time. Not through grand, sweeping gestures, but through the quiet, daily decisions that ultimately define us. Love more deeply. Risk a little more boldly. Listen more carefully. Forgive more generously. These aren't just words—they're invitations to a more intentional life.

My greatest hope is that this book becomes a catalyst. A gentle nudge that reminds you that your life is happening right now, in this moment. And you—yes, you—have the remarkable ability to shape it with purpose, courage, and heart.

Disclaimer

The content of this book is intended for informational and reflective purposes only. It does not constitute legal, financial, medical, or psychological advice and should not be relied upon as a substitute for professional guidance. The insights and reflections contained within are based on common themes of human experience and should not be interpreted as specific recommendations for any individual situation.

Neither the author nor the publisher makes any representations or warranties regarding the accuracy, applicability, or completeness of the information provided. Any decisions, actions, or inactions taken based on the content of this book are the sole responsibility of the reader. The author and publisher disclaim all liability for any direct, indirect, incidental, consequential, or special damages arising from the use, misuse, or inability to use this material, including but not limited to emotional distress, financial losses, health-related decisions, personal relationships, or any other outcomes resulting from actions taken or not taken based on the content of this book. The reader assumes full responsibility for any choices made as a result of engaging with this material.

If you are experiencing distress, mental health concerns, or any medical condition, it is strongly advised that you seek the assistance of a qualified healthcare provider, therapist, or other relevant professional. This book is not intended to diagnose, treat, cure, or prevent any condition and should not replace professional medical or psychological support.

Furthermore, the author and publisher do not assume responsibility for how this book is used, interpreted, or applied by any reader. Any reliance on the information herein is at the reader's own risk. If you are in crisis or require immediate assistance, please seek professional help or contact emergency services.

Your well-being is important. Please use this book as a tool for reflection and self-awareness, but always prioritize professional advice when needed.

Share Your Gained Wisdom

Dear Valued Reader,

Thank you for choosing this book as a guide to reflection and intentional living. Your willingness to explore these 111 common regrets and apply their lessons to your own life is a meaningful step toward a future with fewer regrets.

As an independent author, your feedback is invaluable. Your thoughts not only help others discover this book. If you find this book insightful, we would love to hear from you.

Simply scan the QR code below to leave a review, it only takes a moment but makes a significant impact.

Your support means the world to me, and I am grateful for the opportunity to be part of your journey. Your reviews not only help this book gain exposure but also allow it to reach other readers who might need these insights now more than ever.

With gratitude,

Mauricio

Take Your Reflection Further with the Companion Workbook

This book provides deep insights into the psychological foundations, consequences, and strategies for avoiding life's most common regrets. But understanding regret is just the first step—true transformation happens when you actively reflect, write, and take action.

To help you on this journey, I've created ***The 111 Regrets Reflection Workbook***—a structured guide with 333 powerful questions designed to help you:

✓ Turn insights into personal breakthroughs

✓ Uncover patterns in your life that may lead to regret

✓ Develop an action plan to live with intention

Scan a QR code below to get your copy:

Free Digital Copy → Reflect on-the-go with a downloadable PDF.

Print Version → A physical workbook for writing, journaling, and long-term use.

Your journey to a life with fewer regrets starts now!

Table of Contents

Chapter 1. Introduction

Learned Wisdom: Understanding Regret as a Path to Well-Being

For decades, psychologists and researches have studied human suffering and flourishing, watching as the field of psychology evolved from an exclusive focus on repairing damage to building strength and resilience. Throughout this journey, they have become convinced that our greatest insights often come not from examining perfect lives, but from understanding our deepest regrets and how they might guide us toward more meaningful choices.

When individuals approach the end of life, a remarkable psychological phenomenon occurs: their perceptions crystallize into remarkably consistent patterns of reflection. The non-essential falls away, and what remains are the core truths about what constitutes a well-lived life. This clarity—while valuable at any age—offers particular lessons for those of us still actively constructing our life narratives.

This book presents the 111 most common regrets reported at life's end. Rather than viewing these regrets as merely cautionary tales, I invite you to see them as empirical data points illuminating what humans ultimately find meaningful. By studying these patterns, we can develop what researches call "prospective regret awareness"—the ability to anticipate and avoid choices that undermine long-term well-being.

The Cognitive Architecture of Regret

Research in cognitive psychology has identified two fundamental categories of regret that structure our retrospective thinking:

1. **Regrets of Commission** – Actions we took that we wish we hadn't. These include harsh words spoken impulsively, ethical compromises that violated our values, or persisting in situations we knew were harmful despite warning signals.
2. **Regrets of Omission** – Actions we failed to take that we wish we had. These include dreams never pursued, emotions never expressed, or growth opportunities avoided due to fear or inertia.

A consistent finding across multiple studies is particularly instructive: as people age, regrets of omission consistently outweigh regrets of commission by a significant margin. When researches analyzed the psychological mechanisms underlying this pattern, they discovered a fascinating explanatory factor: humans possess remarkable cognitive abilities to reframe negative actions through rationalization and meaning-making. "That mistake taught me something valuable," we tell ourselves, or "That difficult choice, while painful, made me stronger."

However, our psychological immune system struggles to process what never happened. The unlived possibilities—careers not pursued, relationships not deepened, risks not taken—remain perpetually perfect in imagination precisely because they were never subjected to reality's complications. This creates what psychologists call "opportunity cost regret," which proves remarkably resistant to our normal cognitive defense mechanisms.

As one research participant, an 86-year-old retired teacher, eloquently expressed: "I've made peace with most of my mistakes—they're part of my story now. But I still wonder about the paths I was too afraid to explore. Those haunt me because I'll never know what might have been."

The Six Domains of Life Regret

The systematic analysis of end-of-life regrets reveals a meaningful pattern: they cluster into six distinct domains, each corresponding to fundamental aspects of human flourishing. These aren't arbitrary categories but represent the core dimensions where psychological well-being is either cultivated or compromised through our choices:

1. **Relationships and Connection:** The most frequently cited regrets center on human bonds—time not invested in loved ones, affection unexpressed, conflicts unresolved. "I wish I had told her I loved her more often" or "I should have reconciled with my brother while I had the chance" exemplify this domain. The empirical evidence is unambiguous: across cultures and demographics, the quality of our relationships consistently emerges as the strongest predictor of life satisfaction. When the attachment systems that evolutionary psychology identifies as essential to our species are neglected, profound regret follows almost invariably.

2. **Career and Work-Life Balance:** Research data reveals a striking pattern of regret concerning the allocation of energy between professional pursuits and personal life. "I sacrificed too much family time for work that ultimately didn't matter" represents a common realization. What's particularly noteworthy is that this regret transcends career fields and achievement levels—even those who reached the pinnacle of professional success report similar misgivings about work-life imbalance. The psychological

mechanism appears to involve what behavioral economists call "focusing illusion"—overestimating the impact of career achievements on overall well-being while underestimating the cumulative cost of personal sacrifices.

3. **Personal Growth and Dreams** This domain encompasses regrets about unfulfilled potential and unexplored aspects of identity. "I wish I had pursued my genuine interests rather than taking the safe path" is representative. These regrets align with self-determination theory's emphasis on autonomy and competence as core psychological needs. When individuals persistently suppress authentic interests or avoid growth opportunities due to what psychologists call "safety behaviors" (avoidance of discomfort), they ultimately experience a deficit in what Viktor Frankl termed "self-actualization"—the fulfillment of one's unique potential.

4. **Health and Well-Being** Regrets concerning physical and mental health neglect form another distinct cluster. "I should have taken better care of my body" or "I wish I had addressed my stress earlier" are common expressions. What makes these regrets particularly poignant is their irreversibility—unlike other domains where late corrections remain possible, health consequences often cannot be undone. Research in health psychology demonstrates that we systematically undervalue future health in favor of present convenience, a phenomenon called "temporal discounting" that leads to choices inconsistent with our long-term interests.

5. **Spirituality and Inner Peace** A domain frequently overlooked in conventional psychological research involves regrets about spiritual neglect and inner harmony. "I wish I had spent more time developing inner peace rather than chasing external validation" typifies this category. Empirical studies on contemplative practices and meaning-making reveal that those who cultivate what psychologists call "transcendent self-identity"—a sense of connection to something beyond the individual self—report significantly higher life satisfaction and lower death anxiety. The neglect of this dimension appears to create a distinctive form of existential regret.

6. **Contribution and Legacy** The final domain involves regrets about insufficient impact beyond the self. "I wish I had used my talents to make a meaningful difference for others" represents this category. This aligns with what positive psychology research identifies as "eudemonic well-being"—fulfillment derived from purpose and contribution rather than merely pleasant experiences. When the fundamental human need to matter and to leave

a positive mark remains unfulfilled, a particular quality of regret emerges that centers on legacy and generativity.

What makes these findings especially valuable for constructing a life of meaning is their empirical consistency. These aren't idiosyncratic reflections but representative patterns that emerge across diverse populations. Together, they provide a comprehensive framework—what I call a "well-being blueprint"—for making intentional choices that align with what research tells us humans ultimately find meaningful.

By understanding these six domains, we can develop what is known as "prospective life satisfaction"—the ability to anticipate and cultivate the elements that research consistently associates with a life well-lived. Rather than waiting for the clarity that often comes too late, we can incorporate these insights proactively into our decision-making processes today.

From Regret to Prospective Well-Being

The central premise of positive psychology is that understanding human flourishing allows us to cultivate it deliberately. Similarly, understanding the architecture of regret enables us to restructure our choices proactively.

This book offers more than a catalog of others' sorrows—it provides an evidence-based approach to choosing differently now. Each chapter explores one category of common regrets, examining its psychological foundations, consequences, and practical strategies for making more fulfilling choices.

As you read this book, I encourage you to reflect on your own life choices through these questions:

- Are you investing sufficient attention in relationships that research shows consistently correlate with life satisfaction?
- When making decisions, are you guided by intrinsic values or extrinsic pressures?
- Does your time allocation reflect what you genuinely value, or does it follow patterns you might later regret?
- Are you balancing prudent caution with necessary risk-taking for growth?
- Have you found ways to contribute meaningfully to others' well-being?

These aren't abstract inquiries but practical tools for what I call "regret-minimizing life design." By considering them thoughtfully, you engage in prospective hindsight—imagining your future self looking back on today's choices.

This approach doesn't guarantee a life without mistakes—human choice always involves uncertainty and tradeoffs. However, learning from the consistently reported regrets of others offers us a remarkable opportunity: the chance to incorporate life's most important lessons without having to learn them all firsthand.

Throughout the work of psychology researchers studying human potential, they've observed that what distinguishes a life well-lived isn't the absence of mistakes but the presence of meaning, engagement, positive relationships, achievement, and a sense of purpose. The regrets documented in this book offer a reverse blueprint for these very elements.

In the chapters that follow, we'll explore each domain of common regret systematically, drawing both from the wisdom of those completing their life journey and from psychological research on well-being. My goal is to help you develop what might be called "intentional living"—making choices with full awareness of what ultimately creates a life you can look back upon with satisfaction rather than regret.

The opportunity before us is significant: to learn from others' hindsight while we still have time to shape our own future. Let us approach this exploration not with fear of making mistakes, but with appreciation for the chance to live more authentically, connected, and meaningfully.

Chapter 2. How to Get the Most Out of This Book

Optimizing Your Experience: An Evidence-Based Approach

Throughout the research on human flourishing, studies have observed a fascinating pattern: the way we engage with knowledge matters as much as the knowledge itself. When individuals approach new insights with intentional strategies for integration, their capacity to transform information into meaningful change increases dramatically. This principle applies directly to how you might benefit from the pages that follow.

The regrets documented in this book represent more than anecdotal wisdom—they constitute a remarkable data set on what humans ultimately find meaningful. By applying principles from cognitive psychology and behavior change research, you can transform these insights into what I call "prospective wisdom"—the ability to learn from others' experiences before reaching similar conclusions through your own regrets.

Strategic Engagement Methods

Research on learning and personal transformation suggests several evidence-based approaches to maximize what you gain from this exploration of life's most common regrets:

1. Utilize Selective Engagement

While the book is organized into six thematic domains—relationships, career, personal growth, health, spirituality, and legacy—human experience is rarely compartmentalized so neatly. Studies on adult learning demonstrate that engagement increases substantially when individuals select entry points that align with current concerns or interests.

I recommend beginning with whichever section resonates most strongly with your present life circumstances. If you're navigating career transitions, start there. If relationship questions feel most pressing, begin with those chapters. This selective approach activates what psychologists call "readiness for change"—a state where cognitive and emotional resources are optimally aligned for integration of new insights.

2. Practice Reflective Pause Technique

When you encounter material that creates an emotional response—what psychologists term "cognitive-affective engagement"—resist the urge to continue reading immediately. Instead, implement the "reflective pause technique": stop, breathe mindfully, and ask yourself specific diagnostic questions:

- "What element of this regret feels personally relevant?"
- "Where do I recognize similar patterns in my own choices?"
- "What specific values of mine does this insight highlight?"

This structured reflection transforms passive reading into active psychological processing. Research shows that even brief reflective pauses significantly enhance the integration of insights into behavioral intentions.

3. Employ Future-Self Projection

While regrets originate from the past, their value lies in future application. For each significant insight, engage in what researchers call "episodic future thinking"—a form of mental time travel where you imagine yourself at a future point (perhaps 10 or 20 years ahead) looking back on your current choices.

Ask yourself: "What small, concrete action could I take this week that my future self would thank me for?" This technique leverages temporal self-continuity—connecting your present actions to your future well-being—which consistently predicts positive behavior change across domains.

4. Activate Social Learning Mechanisms

Decades of research in social psychology confirm that learning is dramatically enhanced when it incorporates social interaction. Share specific insights from this book with trusted others, not merely as interesting conversation but as deliberate processing.

When you verbalize what you're learning and receive reflective feedback, you activate multiple cognitive pathways simultaneously. This "multimodal processing" strengthens neural connections and increases the likelihood that insights will translate to behavioral change. Consider forming a small discussion group or engaging a "wisdom partner" with whom you can regularly discuss these life lessons.

5. Implement Structured Documentation

The act of writing about insights creates what psychologists call "cognitive elaboration"—a deeper processing that connects new information to existing knowledge structures. Consider maintaining a "regret prevention journal" where you document:

- Which regrets resonate most strongly
- Specific patterns in your life related to these regrets
- Concrete implementation intentions ("When X occurs, I will do Y")

Research demonstrates that written implementation intentions increase follow-through by approximately 300% compared to mental intentions alone. The specificity of writing creates both clarity and commitment.

6. Cultivate Productive Discomfort

You may notice resistance when encountering certain regrets—a desire to skip ahead or rationalize why they don't apply to you. Research on psychological growth found that this discomfort often signals what we call a "growth edge"—precisely the area where development is most needed.

Rather than avoiding this discomfort, approach it with curious attention. The psychological term "approach motivation" (versus avoidance motivation) describes this willingness to move toward challenging material, which consistently predicts greater psychological flexibility and growth.

7. Practice Self-Compassionate Awareness

As you recognize patterns in your own life that might lead to future regret, apply what psychologists call the "self-compassion framework":

- Acknowledge imperfection as universal human experience (common humanity)
- Observe thoughts and feelings without judgment (mindfulness)
- Extend the same kindness to yourself that you would offer others (self-kindness)

Research by Kristin Neff and others demonstrates that self-compassion—unlike self-criticism—actually increases motivation for meaningful change rather than diminishing it.

A Tool for Intentional Living

The most important concept to understand about this book is that it isn't designed merely to inform, but to transform. The regrets documented here represent the distilled life wisdom of countless individuals who gained clarity through the approach of mortality. By engaging with their insights proactively, you're employing what positive psychology calls "anticipatory learning"—gaining wisdom without paying the full experiential price.

This approach aligns with what researchers have observed throughout decades of research on human potential: those who live meaningfully aren't people who avoid mistakes entirely, but those who develop systematic ways to learn from both their own experiences and others'.

Think of this book not as a passive reading experience but as an active intervention in your life's trajectory—a chance to align your choices today with what consistently matters most when the broader perspective of a life nearing completion comes into view.

In the following chapters, you'll explore specific regrets across six domains of human experience. With each insight, you have the opportunity to ask: "How might this wisdom influence my choices today?" This question represents the essence of intentional living—choosing with awareness of what ultimately creates a life of meaning, connection, and fulfillment.

Chapter 3. Relationships & Connections

1. Not spending enough time with loved ones (family and friends)

This regret exemplifies what behavioral economists call "temporal discounting" – our tendency to undervalue future relationship satisfaction in favor of immediate career rewards. The psychological mechanism is clear: professional achievements provide tangible, immediate feedback (promotions, recognition), while relationship benefits accumulate more subtly but ultimately prove more meaningful to long-term wellbeing.

The Harvard Study of Adult Development, tracking individuals for over 80 years, conclusively demonstrates that relationship quality predicts life satisfaction more reliably than professional success, wealth, or fame. Those who consistently prioritized work over relationships report significantly higher levels of regret in their final years, regardless of career accomplishments attained.

This miscalculation creates what psychologists call an "irreversible opportunity cost" – unlike many life choices that can be amended, time not spent with loved ones who have passed represents a permanent loss that no subsequent action can recover. The emotional impact intensifies as mortality becomes salient, creating a painful clarity about what truly mattered.

Three evidence-based strategies for implementing this wisdom:

1. Create Protected Time Blocks: Research on habit formation shows that scheduling "sacred time" for relationships dramatically increases follow-through. Rather than hoping family time will happen after everything else, schedule it first and protect it with the same vigilance you would your most important work commitment.
2. Conduct Monthly Time Audits: Periodically review how you're allocating hours across different life domains. Studies show that this simple practice often reveals surprising discrepancies between stated values and actual behavior.
3. Apply the "Future Self Test": Before declining family time for work, ask: "Will my future self, looking back, consider this a wise choice?" This technique leverages what psychologists call "prospective hindsight" to make wiser present decisions.

2. Taking loved ones for granted and failing to appreciate them

This pattern exemplifies what psychologists call "hedonic adaptation" – our natural tendency to become accustomed to positive aspects of our lives until they fade from conscious awareness. The psychological mechanism is straightforward: when we first form relationships, the brain's novelty detectors heighten awareness of positive qualities; over time, neurological habituation occurs – what was exceptional becomes expected, reducing our conscious appreciation.

This adaptation isn't a character flaw but a predictable cognitive process. The consequences, however, are significant: studies show that relationships characterized by expressed gratitude demonstrate greater resilience during conflict, enhanced intimacy, and significantly higher longevity than those where appreciation remains implicit.

From a neurobiological perspective, both expressing and receiving appreciation activates reward pathways, releasing oxytocin that strengthens emotional bonds. When appreciation remains unexpressed, these neurochemical benefits go unrealized for both parties, creating a subtle but cumulative relationship deficit.

Three evidence-based strategies to counter hedonic adaptation:

1. Implement Appreciation Rituals: Studies show that institutionalizing gratitude through regular practices significantly increases expression by over 300%. Consider establishing daily or weekly moments dedicated specifically to acknowledging others' positive contributions.

2. Practice Appreciation Specificity: Research demonstrates that concrete, detailed appreciation creates stronger positive effects than general statements. Rather than "thanks for everything," identify particular actions or qualities: "I really appreciate how attentively you listened when I was struggling yesterday."

3. Set Environmental Reminders: Simple cues like phone notifications or strategically placed notes effectively interrupt adaptation patterns. These external prompts compensate for the natural decline in appreciation awareness, ensuring consistent expression despite psychological habituation.

3. Not expressing love and affection openly to those who mattered

This regret reflects what communication researchers call "emotional expressiveness asymmetry" – the gap between felt emotions and their verbal or physical expression. Research consistently shows that individuals feel affection more frequently than they express it, creating a disconnect that significantly impacts relationship quality.

The psychological barrier to expression often stems from what attachment theorists term "vulnerability avoidance" – protecting ourselves from potential rejection by withholding emotional disclosure. Neuroimaging studies reveal that vulnerability activates the same brain regions as physical threat detection, explaining why emotional expression can feel genuinely risky despite its relational benefits.

The consequences extend beyond relationship satisfaction to physical wellbeing. Controlled studies demonstrate that individuals who regularly express positive emotions show lower blood pressure, reduced stress hormones, and enhanced immune function compared to those who habitually withhold emotional expression – suggesting that suppression has physiological costs.

Three evidence-based strategies to enhance emotional expression:

1. Start with Lower-Risk Modalities: Research shows that written expressions often feel safer than verbal ones for individuals with expression discomfort. Begin with notes or messages before progressing to direct verbal expression if this represents a challenge.
2. Practice "Expression Expansion": Psychological studies demonstrate that starting with comfortable phrases and gradually expanding your emotional vocabulary creates sustainable change. Each small step builds capacity for the next.
3. Utilize Natural Transition Points: Research on habit formation shows that linking expression to daily transitions (morning greetings, departures, bedtime) dramatically increases consistency by embedding new behaviors within existing routines.

4. Not saying "I love you" enough to my family and friends

This specific regret exemplifies what psychologists call "assumed knowledge error" – the mistaken belief that others automatically know our feelings without explicit verbalization. Research shows consistent perception gaps in relationships, with recipients reporting greater uncertainty about being loved than expressers anticipate.

Developmental research reveals that the phrase "I love you" serves a unique psychological function beyond general affection. Neuroimaging studies demonstrate that hearing these specific words activates attachment centers in the brain that process security and belonging in ways that nonverbal expressions alone cannot replicate – explaining why "showing" love doesn't fully substitute for stating it directly.

The reluctance to verbalize love often stems from what relationship researchers call "emotional risk assessment" – subconsciously weighing vulnerability against potential rejection. This caution frequently originates in formative experiences where emotional openness led to disappointment, creating lasting hesitation despite changed circumstances.

Three evidence-based strategies to increase comfort with love expression:

1. Implement Expression Scheduling: Research shows that planning specific occasions for expression reduces anticipatory anxiety while increasing follow-through. Identify natural opportunities when expression would feel most authentic.
2. Recognize Individual Differences: Studies on "love languages" confirm that verbal affirmation matters more to some individuals than others. Understanding your recipient's preferences allows targeted expression that meets their specific emotional needs.
3. Create Environmental Triggers: Simple reminders effectively interrupt habits of verbal restraint. Associate existing daily activities (like morning coffee or commuting) with brief moments of expression to build sustainable patterns.

5. Not apologizing or making amends when I hurt someone dear

This regret reflects what conflict researchers call "repair avoidance" – postponing reconciliation due to pride, fear, or discomfort with vulnerability. The psychological mechanism involves what cognitive therapists identify as "ego-protective distortions" – mental frameworks that prioritize self-image preservation over relationship restoration.

Several cognitive biases reinforce this tendency: "catastrophizing" leads us to overestimate the emotional risks of initiating reconciliation; "mind-reading" convinces us we know how others will respond without verification; "all-or-nothing thinking" frames apologizing as complete capitulation rather than relationship investment.

The consequences extend beyond relationship damage to personal wellbeing. Studies demonstrate that harboring unresolved conflicts correlates with increased cardiovascular risk, compromised immune function, and elevated stress hormones. The psychological burden manifests physically, creating what researchers term "embodied resentment."

Three evidence-based strategies to overcome reconciliation barriers:

1. Practice Psychological Time-Travel: Research demonstrates that considering conflicts from a future perspective (imagining how they'll appear five years ahead) facilitates more constructive responses. This temporal distancing reduces immediate emotional intensity.
2. Utilize the Components of Effective Apology: Relationship science identifies specific elements of successful reconciliation: acknowledging specific harm, expressing genuine remorse, offering appropriate reparation, and committing to changed behavior. This structure increases effectiveness.
3. Recognize Reconciliation as Self-Benefit: Studies show that initiating reconciliation provides psychological benefits regardless of the recipient's response. Framing apology as personal growth rather than social risk enhances motivation.

6. Holding onto grudges and not forgiving loved ones

This regret exemplifies what forgiveness researchers call "resentment persistence" – maintaining negative emotional states toward others long after the precipitating events. The psychological mechanism reflects our brain's negativity bias, which evolved to protect us from threats but creates disproportionate focus on past injuries.

Neuroimaging studies reveal why grudge-holding feels like carrying a weight; it literally requires ongoing neural resources. Brain scans show that actively maintaining grudges activates regions associated with negative affect, stress response, and cognitive control – essentially requiring continual psychological effort to sustain.

The health consequences are well-documented. Meta-analyses of forgiveness research demonstrate that individuals who maintain grudges show higher blood pressure, increased cortisol levels, compromised immune function, and greater vulnerability to depression compared to those who practice forgiveness. What begins as emotional self-protection transforms into physiological self-harm over time.

Three evidence-based strategies to facilitate forgiveness:

1. Reconceptualize Forgiveness: Research shows that defining forgiveness as emotional release rather than relationship restoration makes it more psychologically accessible. Forgiveness primarily benefits the forgiver regardless of relationship outcomes.

2. Practice Perspective-Taking: Studies demonstrate that attempting to understand contextual factors influencing the offender's behavior reduces attribution of malicious intent, facilitating forgiveness without excusing harmful actions.

3. Implement Expressive Writing: Controlled studies show that structured writing about emotional wounds accelerates processing and release. Articulating both the injury and its impact creates cognitive organization that facilitates resolution.

7. Not forgiving myself for mistakes that hurt my relationships

This regret highlights what psychologists term "self-compassion deficit" – the tendency to extend greater understanding and forgiveness to others than to ourselves. Research demonstrates that self-criticism activates threat-response neural circuits, triggering stress hormones that impair cognitive flexibility and emotional regulation – precisely when we most need these capacities.

The psychological roots often lie in what developmental psychologists call "internalized standards rigidity" – absorbing perfectionist expectations that become more stringently applied to ourselves than to others. This creates a double standard where others' mistakes are seen as human while our own become defining character indictments.

The consequences extend beyond emotional well-being to relationship functioning. Research shows that individuals struggling with self-forgiveness demonstrate greater defensiveness, reduced empathy, and impaired conflict resolution skills – the psychological weight of carried guilt compromises present relationship capacity.

Three evidence-based strategies to develop self-forgiveness:

1. Practice Common Humanity Recognition: Research by Kristin Neff demonstrates that acknowledging the universality of mistakes reduces shame and facilitates self-compassion. Recognizing that error is an inevitable aspect of being human creates psychological space for growth.

2. Implement Future-Self Behavior Change: Studies show that coupling self-forgiveness with specific commitments to different future actions creates healthier resolution than ongoing self-punishment. This forward orientation promotes growth rather than rumination.

3. Distinguish Responsibility from Identity: Psychological research indicates that separating "I made a mistake" from "I am a mistake" significantly enhances capacity for constructive change. This cognitive reframing prevents harmful self-definition through past actions.

8. Losing touch with close friends over the years

This regret reflects what social network researchers call "relationship entropy" – the natural tendency of connections to weaken over time without active maintenance. Unlike family relationships, which often have institutional and structural support, friendships rely almost entirely on voluntary investment that competes with other life demands.

The psychological mechanism involves what economists term "present bias" – our tendency to prioritize immediate responsibilities over long-term investments, even when the latter offer greater returns. When facing competing priorities, friendship maintenance often falls to the bottom of our priority list despite its documented importance for wellbeing.

The consequences emerge most clearly in later life stages. Studies demonstrate that friendship network breadth and quality in older adulthood strongly predict cognitive health, physical wellbeing, and longevity – sometimes more powerfully than family relationships due to their voluntary nature.

Three evidence-based strategies to maintain friendship connections:

1. Implement Friendship Maintenance Scheduling: Research shows that institutionalizing connection through regular rituals significantly increases relationship longevity. Create recurring contact points (monthly calls, annual gatherings) to maintain bonds despite life transitions.

2. Develop Transition Strategies: Studies demonstrate that proactively planning friendship maintenance during major life changes (relocation, parenthood, career shifts) dramatically increases relationship preservation when natural drift would otherwise occur.

3. Utilize Technology Strategically: Research indicates that different communication methods serve distinct relationship functions. Match your approach to your goal: text messages maintain awareness, voice calls strengthen emotional connection, and video interactions build presence.

9. Not being fully present when spending time with family

This regret exemplifies what attention researchers call "continuous partial attention" – being physically present while mentally elsewhere. The psychological pattern reflects our increasingly fragmented attention environment, where competing cognitive demands create habitual divided awareness.

Neurobiological research explains why divided attention undermines connection quality. Meaningful engagement activates "mirror neuron systems" that create neural synchronization between individuals – essentially allowing two brains to align their activity patterns. This synchronization requires sustained attentional focus and fails under conditions of distraction.

The consequences appear in both relationship satisfaction and developmental research. Studies with parent-child dyads demonstrate that even brief periods of parental distraction during interactions significantly reduces connection quality and child sense of importance. Similar patterns emerge in adult relationships, where perceived partner responsiveness – feeling truly seen and heard – serves as a central predictor of relationship satisfaction.

Three evidence-based strategies to enhance attentional quality:

1. Create Technology Boundaries: Research demonstrates that visible devices (even when not in use) significantly reduce connection quality and conversation depth. Establish device-free zones or periods to protect interaction quality.
2. Practice Attentional Reset Rituals: Studies show that brief mindfulness exercises effectively clear "attention residue" from previous tasks. Before family interactions, implement a brief mental reset to transition fully into the present moment.
3. Develop Uni-tasking Capacity: Contrary to popular belief, multitasking represents a cognitive impossibility. Practice deliberate uni-tasking – doing just one thing with full attention – to strengthen your capacity for sustained presence.

10. Putting work or other obligations before family time

This regret reflects what economists call "opportunity cost neglect" – our tendency to focus on the gains of chosen activities without fully accounting for what we sacrifice. When deciding between work and family time, we naturally emphasize work completion benefits rather than the cumulative cost of missed connections.

From an evolutionary perspective, humans developed in environments where status and resource acquisition directly impacted survival. Our psychological architecture still responds to these drives, even when contemporary circumstances have transformed their relative importance to wellbeing.

The consequences emerge both immediately and cumulatively. Research demonstrates that excessive work hours correlate with increased relationship conflict, reduced intimacy, and higher dissolution rates. Children of chronically overworking parents show higher rates of behavioral problems, reduced security, and weakened attachment – creating intergenerational impact.

Three evidence-based strategies for healthier work-life integration:

1. Reject False Dichotomy Thinking: Research demonstrates that conceptualizing work and relationships as competing priorities creates unnecessary conflict. Instead, seek integration opportunities – bringing family into work contexts occasionally or sharing work experiences with family appropriately.
2. Practice Values-Based Scheduling: Explicitly aligning time allocation with stated priorities significantly reduces value-behavior discrepancies. Regular calendar reviews ensure that time investment reflects genuine priorities rather than default patterns.
3. Implement Presence Transitions: Studies show that creating deliberate psychological shifts between work and family roles significantly enhances engagement quality. Develop brief rituals (changing clothes, short walks, mindfulness moments) that facilitate complete attention transitions.

11. Not being a better spouse or partner (lack of effort, understanding, or commitment)

This regret exemplifies what relationship researchers call "maintenance neglect" – the tendency to underinvest in partnership quality during non-crisis periods. Research demonstrates that successful long-term relationships don't simply persist; they require consistent attentional investment, much like a garden needs regular tending rather than occasional intensive care.

The psychological underpinning involves what social scientists term "security complacency" – the assumption that relationship stability equals relationship health. Studies by John Gottman reveal that flourishing partnerships maintain a 5:1 ratio of positive to negative interactions, creating an "emotional bank account" that sustains connection through inevitable challenges. When this ratio drops, relationships gradually experience emotional distancing that becomes increasingly difficult to reverse.

The consequences manifest both emotionally and physiologically. Research demonstrates that marital dissatisfaction correlates with elevated inflammatory markers, stress hormones, and cardiovascular reactivity – suggesting that relationship quality directly impacts physical health. Moreover, the awareness of having undervalued one's partner creates what attachment theorists call "relationship remorse" – a particularly painful form of regret centered on irretrievable interpersonal opportunities.

Three evidence-based strategies for partnership investment:

1. Implement Attunement Practice: Gottman's research identifies daily "bids for connection" – small opportunities to respond to your partner's needs or interests. Deliberately turning toward these bids rather than away from them significantly predicts relationship longevity.
2. Establish Appreciation Rituals: Studies show that regularly expressing specific gratitude for your partner's qualities or actions creates a positive feedback loop that enhances relationship satisfaction for both parties.
3. Prioritize Stress Buffering: Research confirms that actively helping your partner navigate stressors through emotional support strengthens secure attachment and psychological safety – foundational elements of partnership satisfaction.

12. Not being a better parent (missing important moments in my children's lives)

This regret reflects what developmental psychologists call "critical period oversight" – undervaluing time-limited opportunities for connection and influence during crucial developmental windows. The psychological mechanism involves what economists term "parental time inconsistency" – the tendency to overweight immediate professional demands while undervaluing long-term relationship investments with children.

Research by developmental psychologists demonstrates that parental presence creates "emotional contingency" – the sense that a child's experiences and emotions matter and are responded to appropriately. This contingency forms the foundation for secure attachment, which studies link to better emotional regulation, healthier relationships, and greater psychological resilience throughout life.

The consequences of missed parental connection opportunities accumulate in what family systems theorists call "relational absence" – an emotional distance that becomes increasingly difficult to bridge as children develop autonomy. Parents approaching life's end often recognize that these windows for formative connection cannot be retrospectively accessed, creating profound regret over irreversible relational opportunities.

Three evidence-based strategies for parental presence:

1. Practice Special Time: Research shows that even brief periods of undivided attention (10-15 minutes) with complete child-directed focus significantly enhance attachment security and perceived parental availability.
2. Establish Emotion Coaching: Studies by John Gottman demonstrate that parents who validate emotions rather than dismissing them raise children with better emotional intelligence and stronger parent-child bonds.
3. Create Developmental Rituals: Research shows that predictable routines around transition periods (bedtime, meals, milestones) provide children with security while creating memory anchors that strengthen family identity and connection across time.

13. Not being a better son or daughter (neglecting my parents when they needed me)

This regret exemplifies what family psychologists call "filial responsibility neglect" – the failure to reciprocate the care and support received in earlier life stages. The psychological mechanism involves "generational myopia" – difficulty seeing parents as individuals with emotional needs rather than primarily as caregivers.

Research in intergenerational equity demonstrates that reciprocal care strengthens not only relationship quality but also psychological well-being for both parties. Adult children who actively support aging parents report greater purpose and meaning, while parents experience reduced depression and greater life satisfaction through maintained connection. This mutual benefit reflects what social scientists call "generativity fulfillment" – meeting the developmental need to contribute to the next generation while honoring the previous one.

The consequences of parental neglect create what gerontologists term "late-life relationship poverty" – missed opportunities for wisdom transmission, shared experiences, and meaningful closure before death. The growing awareness of this relational deficit often intensifies as mortality approaches, creating a particularly poignant form of retrospective regret.

Three evidence-based strategies for honoring aging parents:

1. Practice Life Review Interviews: Research shows that deliberately soliciting parents' stories and experiences creates meaningful connection while preserving family history that would otherwise be lost.
2. Implement Structured Contact: Studies demonstrate that establishing regular communication rhythms (weekly calls, monthly visits) significantly increases relationship satisfaction compared to sporadic, crisis-driven contact.
3. Develop Collaborative Care Planning: Research indicates that involving parents in discussions about their needs and preferences, rather than making unilateral decisions, enhances their sense of dignity and autonomy while strengthening family bonds.

14. Allowing pride or fear to prevent me from saving an important relationship

This regret illustrates what social psychologists call "reconciliation avoidance" – allowing ego protection to outweigh relationship restoration. The psychological foundation involves what researchers term "face threat" – the perceived risk to self-image that accompanies admitting error or initiating repair after conflict.

Research in relationship science reveals that successful repair attempts follow a predictable pattern: vulnerability, accountability, and behavioral commitment. When pride or fear prevents this sequence, relationships remain in what John Gottman calls "emotional gridlock" – a state of unresolved tension that gradually erodes connection quality.

The consequences of unrepaired relationships manifest both psychologically and physiologically. Studies demonstrate that unresolved interpersonal conflict correlates with elevated stress hormones, compromised immune function, and rumination – creating what health psychologists call "embodied resentment" that affects physical well-being. Moreover, the awareness of having sacrificed potentially fulfilling relationships for ego protection creates what meaning-focused therapists identify as "values-behavior incongruence" – a significant source of end-of-life regret.

Three evidence-based strategies for relationship repair:

1. Practice Psychological Time Travel: Research shows that adopting a distant future perspective ("How will this matter in five years?") reduces defensive responses and facilitates reconciliation by highlighting long-term relationship value over short-term ego protection.
2. Implement Graduated Contact: Studies demonstrate that rebuilding connection through progressively increasing engagement (written communication before in-person meetings) reduces anxiety and increases repair success.
3. Apply Vulnerability First: Relationship science confirms that initiating reconciliation with genuine disclosure of feelings rather than accusations dramatically increases receptiveness in the other party, creating psychological safety for mutual repair.

15. Letting a true love slip away and not fighting for that relationship

This regret exemplifies what decision researchers call "status quo bias" – favoring inaction over action even when the potential benefits of change outweigh the risks. The psychological mechanism involves what behavioral economists term "loss aversion" – our tendency to fear potential relationship pain more acutely than we anticipate relationship joy.

This cognitive distortion leads to what attachment theorists identify as "commitment hesitation" – reluctance to fully invest in promising relationships due to uncertainty or fear. Research demonstrates that successful long-term couples typically weren't certain about their relationship's perfect fit initially but rather chose commitment despite normal uncertainty, gradually building deep connection through investment rather than waiting for perfect certainty before investing.

The consequences of abandoned relationship potential create what meaning-focused psychologists call "path-not-taken regret" – a particularly persistent form of counterfactual thinking that intensifies rather than diminishes with time. Unlike regrets of action, which benefit from psychological immune system processes that justify our choices, regrets of relationship inaction remain "perfect possibilities" in imagination, creating especially poignant end-of-life reflection.

Three evidence-based strategies for relationship courage:

1. Practice Values Clarification: Research shows that explicitly identifying what matters most to you in relationships helps overcome fear-based avoidance by connecting choices to deeper meaning rather than emotional comfort.
2. Implement Risk Reframing: Studies demonstrate that conceptualizing vulnerability not as danger but as necessary for connection significantly increases willingness to take emotional risks that deepen relationships.
3. Apply Regret Forecasting: Research indicates that imagining how you might feel about relationship decisions from a future perspective reduces present hesitation and facilitates commitment to potentially meaningful connections.

16. Not having the courage to open my heart fully to love (fear of vulnerability)

This regret reflects what attachment researchers call "intimacy avoidance" – maintaining emotional distance as protection against potential rejection or abandonment. The psychological foundation involves what neuroscientists have identified as "vulnerability threat response" – the activation of the same brain regions during emotional exposure as during physical danger, creating genuine distress that feels reasonable to avoid.

This protective mechanism typically develops through what developmental psychologists term "attachment injury" – early experiences where emotional openness led to rejection or invalidation, creating lasting hesitation despite changed circumstances. Research demonstrates that these protective barriers, while intended to prevent pain, paradoxically create what relationship scientists call "connection poverty" – a state of relative emotional isolation despite physical proximity.

The consequences extend beyond relationship quality to physical wellbeing. Studies show that individuals who maintain emotional barriers demonstrate higher allostatic load (cumulative stress markers), increased inflammatory markers, and reduced immune function compared to those with secure attachment patterns – suggesting that heart protection carries literal cardiovascular costs.

Three evidence-based strategies for developing vulnerability courage:

1. Practice Graduated Disclosure: Research shows that systematically sharing increasingly personal information in manageable steps builds vulnerability tolerance while minimizing anxiety.
2. Implement Self-Compassion Protocols: Studies by Kristin Neff demonstrate that self-kindness during moments of emotional risk significantly reduces fear of rejection and facilitates greater interpersonal openness.
3. Develop Secure-Base Relationships: Attachment research indicates that building trust gradually with select individuals creates psychological safety that generalizes to other relationships, gradually expanding capacity for emotional openness.

17. Not reaching out to reconcile with estranged family members or friends sooner

This regret exemplifies what relationship researchers call "reengagement procrastination" – indefinitely postponing reconciliation attempts due to discomfort, pride, or assumed futility. The psychological mechanism involves what decision scientists term "uncertainty aversion" – preferring the known discomfort of estrangement over the unpredictable outcome of reconciliation attempts.

This avoidance pattern reflects our brain's negativity bias – our tendency to anticipate and overweight potential negative outcomes while underestimating resilience and positive possibilities. Research demonstrates that most relationship ruptures are more reparable than anticipated, yet we systematically overestimate the likelihood of rejection and underestimate the potential for healing.

The consequences of prolonged estrangement create what family systems theorists call "emotional amputation" – the loss of potentially nurturing connections that might otherwise provide support, meaning, and belonging. As mortality becomes salient, this awareness intensifies into what gerontologists identify as "reconciliation urgency" – the heightened desire to resolve relational ruptures before death makes resolution impossible.

Three evidence-based strategies for relationship reconciliation:

1. Implement Expectation Management: Research shows that approaching reconciliation as a process rather than an event, with modest initial goals focused on communication rather than immediate closeness, significantly increases success rates.
2. Practice Perspective-Taking: Studies demonstrate that deliberately considering the other person's experience of the estrangement reduces defensive positioning and facilitates empathic connection necessary for genuine repair.
3. Utilize Written Initiation: Research indicates that thoughtfully composed letters or emails often prove more effective than spontaneous verbal approaches, allowing careful consideration of tone while giving the recipient space to process before responding.

18. Causing pain to loved ones through my actions and not making it right

This regret reflects what moral psychologists call "remediation avoidance" – failing to take responsibility for interpersonal harm due to shame, defensiveness, or discomfort. The psychological mechanism involves what relationship researchers term "accountability threat" – the ego challenge of acknowledging that our actions negatively impacted someone we care about.

This avoidance pattern stems from what cognitive scientists identify as "fundamental attribution error in reverse" – attributing our harmful actions to temporary external circumstances while failing to recognize their lasting impact on others. Research demonstrates that unaddressed harm creates what trauma specialists call "betrayal injury" – a particular form of relationship wound that erodes trust and security in proportion to the closeness of the relationship.

The consequences manifest in a phenomenon attachment researchers have thoroughly documented – the gradual diminishment of psychological safety within relationships that should provide comfort and security. This erosion affects not only the specific relationship but also one's overall sense of moral integrity, producing a well-established pattern meaning-focused psychological studies have identified – behavior inconsistent with one's deepest values.

Three evidence-based strategies for effective repair:

1. Implement Complete Apology Protocol: Research identifies five components of effective apologies: acknowledgment of specific harm, expression of genuine remorse, explanation without excuse, reparation offer, and behavior change commitment. Including all components significantly increases healing potential.

2. Practice Shame Management: Studies show that distinguishing shame ("I am bad") from guilt ("I did something bad") dramatically increases willingness to address harm, as guilt motivates repair while shame promotes avoidance.

3. Develop Amends Orientation: Research demonstrates that conceptualizing repair as an ongoing process rather than a single conversation creates sustainable behavioral change that rebuilds trust over time through consistent demonstration of changed patterns.

19. Not supporting or encouraging my loved ones' dreams and goals

This regret exemplifies what developmental psychologists call "validation neglect" – failing to affirm others' aspirations and potential, particularly when we hold influential roles in their lives. The psychological mechanism involves what cognitive scientists term "possibility blindness" – difficulty envisioning success paths different from our own experiences or expectations.

This limitation reflects a well-documented tendency in human cognition – assuming others share our risk assessments, values hierarchies, and definitions of success. Research demonstrates that receiving encouragement serves as an essential psychological resource that fundamentally expands perceived possibilities and sustains motivation through inevitable challenges – a finding consistently verified across multiple studies in developmental and positive psychology.

The consequences of withheld encouragement create what developmental researchers call "confidence corrosion" – the gradual diminishment of self-efficacy that occurs when significant others express doubt rather than support. This impact grows exponentially with relational importance; criticism from those we love affects us more powerfully than from those with whom we share less attachment.

Three evidence-based strategies for supportive encouragement:

1. Practice Growth Mindset Reflection: Research by Carol Dweck demonstrates that focusing encouragement on effort and strategy rather than innate talent significantly increases persistence and resilience in goal pursuit.

2. Implement Specific Affirmation: Studies show that identifying particular strengths or capacities you observe in others creates more meaningful encouragement than general praise, providing concrete evidence of potential.

3. Develop What-If Exploration: Research indicates that curious questioning about possibilities rather than immediate problem-identification creates psychological safety for dream-sharing while building collaborative problem-solving rather than discouragement.

20. Failing to create special memories or traditions with my family

This regret highlights what family systems researchers call "ritual neglect" – underinvestment in the structured, repeating experiences that build family identity and cohesion. The psychological foundation involves what developmental scientists term "memory anchoring" – the way shared experiences, particularly those with emotional significance, create reference points that strengthen relational bonds across time.

Research demonstrates that family rituals serve multiple psychological functions: they provide predictability that enhances security, create shared meaning that builds group identity, and establish intergenerational continuity that connects family members across time. When these structured traditions are absent, families experience what sociologists call "narrative thinness" – a relative poverty of shared stories and experiences that define "who we are together."

The consequences extend beyond immediate emotional connection to long-term psychological outcomes. Studies reveal that children raised in families with consistent rituals demonstrate greater resilience, stronger identity formation, and higher relationship satisfaction in adulthood – suggesting that these shared experiences create developmental assets that benefit individuals throughout life.

Three evidence-based strategies for meaningful memory creation:

1. Implement Intentional Traditions: Research shows that even simple, consistent rituals (special birthday celebrations, holiday customs, weekly family dinners) create disproportionately powerful memory imprints and family identity.

2. Practice Experience Investment: Studies demonstrate that allocating resources toward shared experiences rather than material acquisitions yields significantly greater and more lasting happiness returns.

3. Develop Memory Capture Methods: Research indicates that documenting experiences through photographs, journals, or storytelling enhances their psychological impact by creating opportunities for reminiscence that reinforces shared identity and connection.

21. Staying too long in an unhealthy or toxic relationship instead of leaving sooner

This regret exemplifies what behavioral economists call "sunk cost fallacy" – continuing investment in a detrimental situation due to resources already expended rather than future prospects. The psychological mechanism involves what relationship scientists term "commitment persistence" – maintaining attachment despite evidence of harm due to identity investment, fear of uncertainty, or misplaced loyalty.

This pattern often reflects what trauma specialists identify as "learned helplessness" – the gradual erosion of perceived agency that occurs through repeated experiences of invalidation or control. Research demonstrates that toxic relationships create neurobiological adaptations similar to addiction – including intermittent reinforcement patterns and biochemical dependency that make separation psychologically and physically challenging despite clear evidence of harm.

The consequences manifest in what health psychologists call "allostatic overload" – the cumulative physiological impact of chronic stress that affects cardiovascular, immune, and neurological functioning. Beyond physical effects, remaining in harmful relationships creates what identity researchers term "self-concept distortion" – the gradual internalization of negative messages that fundamentally alters one's sense of worth and capability.

Three evidence-based strategies for healthier relationship decisions:

1. Implement Values-Based Assessment: Research shows that explicitly evaluating relationships against personally identified values rather than emotions or history significantly clarifies decision-making in ambivalent situations.

2. Practice Support Mobilization: Studies demonstrate that cultivating connections outside the problematic relationship dramatically increases capacity to make difficult transitions by providing both practical assistance and perspective.

3. Develop Worth Reclamation: Research indicates that deliberate reconnection with personal strengths, interests, and capabilities outside the relationship context creates psychological resources necessary for separation from identity-eroding dynamics.

Chapter 4. Career & Work-Life Balance

22. Working too much and missing out on life's important moments

This regret exemplifies what psychologists call "temporal allocation error" – our tendency to systematically misallocate time away from what provides lasting fulfillment. The psychological mechanism is revealing: we confuse instrumental goals (career advancement) with terminal goals (happiness, connection), forgetting that the former are merely means to the latter.

Research in positive psychology demonstrates this miscalculation has neurobiological roots. Our brain's reward circuits provide immediate feedback for work accomplishments but more subtle, cumulative rewards for relationship experiences. In studies tracking thousands of individuals across decades, relationship quality consistently emerges as the strongest predictor of life satisfaction – far outweighing professional achievements that seemed momentarily crucial.

The consequences of work-dominated time allocation create what I call "connection deficit disorder" – the progressive weakening of social bonds that occurs when relationships receive only residual attention. Unlike material resources, time exhibits perfect scarcity – it cannot be recovered, borrowed, or replaced once spent. This irreversibility intensifies the psychological impact of allocation errors, creating what existential psychologists term "retrospective void" – the painful awareness of absence in life's most meaningful domains.

Three evidence-based strategies for wiser temporal investment:

1. Implement Values-Based Time Budgeting: Research demonstrates that explicitly allocating time to relationships proportionate to their stated importance dramatically reduces value-behavior discrepancies.
2. Practice Mindful Presence: Studies show that fully engaging during family time—without digital distractions or mental preoccupation with work—creates relationship benefits disproportionate to the time invested.

3. Adopt Time Sufficiency Mindset: Psychological research confirms that reconceptualizing time as abundant rather than scarce significantly enhances both generosity with time and subsequent satisfaction with time allocation decisions.

23. Putting career and success ahead of family and personal life

This regret reflects what positive psychologists call "dimensional neglect" – developing one aspect of well-being (achievement) while systematically underinvesting in others (relationships, meaning, positive emotion). The psychological foundation involves what economists term "focusing illusion" – overestimating the impact of professional success on overall happiness while underestimating adaptation effects.

Research consistently demonstrates that extrinsic achievements (wealth, status, recognition) provide surprisingly modest and short-lived boosts to subjective well-being compared to relationship quality. The brain's remarkable adaptation system quickly neutralizes positive emotions from achievement, creating what psychologists call the "hedonic treadmill" – requiring ever-greater accomplishments to maintain the same satisfaction level.

The consequences manifest in what we've identified as "domain atrophy" – the gradual diminishment of capacity for joy, connection, and meaning when these dimensions receive insufficient attention. Interestingly, Studies reveal that individuals who maintain balanced life investments report not only greater well-being but also superior long-term career sustainability – suggesting that balance enhances rather than hinders professional success.

Three evidence-based strategies for dimensional balance:

1. Practice PERMA Portfolio Management: Research shows that deliberately cultivating all five well-being dimensions (Positive emotion, Engagement, Relationships, Meaning, Achievement) creates significantly greater life satisfaction than excellence in any single domain.
2. Implement Non-Negotiable Scheduling: Studies demonstrate that establishing inviolable time blocks for family and personal renewal dramatically improves both relationship quality and professional creativity.
3. Develop Success Metric Diversification: Psychological research confirms that measuring achievement across multiple life domains rather than exclusively through career advancement creates both greater resilience and life satisfaction.

24. Staying in a job I disliked out of comfort or fear of change

This regret illustrates what decision scientists call "anticipated regret asymmetry" – systematically overestimating potential regret from action while underestimating regret from inaction. The psychological mechanism involves what neuroscientists term "negativity dominance" – our brain's tendency to give greater weight to potential negative outcomes than positive ones when facing uncertainty.

This evolutionary adaptation, which once protected our ancestors from physical threats, creates a decisional landscape biased toward maintaining unsatisfying status quo conditions rather than risking change. Research in affective forecasting shows we consistently overestimate how badly we'll feel if changes don't work out while underestimating our remarkable psychological immune system – our capacity to find meaning and adapt to new circumstances.

The consequences extend beyond temporary dissatisfaction to what positive psychologists call "learned helplessness transference" – gradually diminishing belief in our agency across multiple life domains. Studies demonstrate that prolonged exposure to controllable negative circumstances creates neural patterns of passivity that generalize beyond the original context, affecting overall psychological functioning.

Three evidence-based strategies for overcoming inertia:

1. Practice Prospective Autobiography: Research shows that writing about your life from a future perspective dramatically clarifies which present choices you're likely to regret, reducing status quo bias.
2. Implement Risk Portfolio Diversification: Studies demonstrate that making several smaller career changes before major transitions significantly increases confidence while providing valuable information about preferences and capacities.
3. Cultivate Growth Mindset Orientation: Psychological research confirms that viewing challenges as learning opportunities rather than threats to self-worth dramatically enhances willingness to embrace beneficial change despite uncertainty.

25. Not pursuing the career path or dream job I truly wanted

This regret exemplifies what vocational psychologists call "authentic alignment deficit" – the gap between one's deeply held interests and actual career path. The psychological foundation involves what motivation researchers term "internalization failure" – adopting external definitions of success rather than identifying personally meaningful goals.

Research demonstrates that career decisions based predominantly on extrinsic factors (salary, prestige, others' expectations) correlate with significantly lower work satisfaction and higher regret intensity than choices aligned with intrinsic motivation. This pattern reflects our fundamental psychological need for autonomy – experiencing ourselves as authors of our life narrative rather than passive characters in others' scripts.

The consequences manifest in what positive psychologists call "engagement deficit" – the absence of flow experiences that emerge when activities align with personal strengths and interests. Studies reveal that individuals working in misaligned careers demonstrate not only lower job satisfaction but also elevated rates of depression, physical illness, and substance abuse – suggesting misalignment creates cumulative psychological and physiological costs.

Three evidence-based strategies for authentic career alignment:

1. Implement Strengths-Based Career Design: Research shows that identifying signature strengths through validated assessments and deliberately seeking opportunities to apply them significantly increases work engagement and meaning.
2. Practice Values Clarification: Studies demonstrate that explicitly identifying core personal values and using them as decision criteria rather than external metrics dramatically enhances career satisfaction.
3. Develop Possible Selves Exploration: Psychological research confirms that systematically investigating various career identities through information gathering, shadowing, and limited experimentation provides crucial data for authentic vocational choices.

26. Not taking risks or making bold moves in my career when I had the chance

This regret reflects what decision scientists call "omission bias" – our tendency to judge errors of inaction as less blameworthy than errors of action, despite potentially greater long-term costs. The psychological mechanism involves what neuroscientists term "uncertainty aversion" – the brain's threat response activates more strongly facing ambiguous outcomes than even known negative ones.

Research by psychologist Thomas Gilovich reveals a fascinating temporal pattern: while action regrets initially feel more intense, inaction regrets grow stronger over time and ultimately dominate end-of-life reflections. This occurs because our psychological immune system effectively processes action regrets ("I learned from that mistake") but struggles with paths not taken, which remain perfect in imagination.

The consequences extend beyond specific opportunities to what identity researchers call "narrative foreclosure" – prematurely concluding that one's life story is complete and can no longer evolve. Studies demonstrate that individuals who periodically embrace calculated risks report greater vitality, psychological growth, and ultimately life satisfaction than those whose decisions are primarily security-oriented.

Three evidence-based strategies for judicious risk-taking:

1. Practice Regret Minimization Framework: Research confirms that decisions evaluated through the lens of minimizing future regret ("Which choice might I most regret not taking?") significantly enhance long-term satisfaction with outcomes.
2. Implement Challenge Network Development: Studies show that cultivating relationships with individuals who supportively question our assumptions dramatically improves decision quality when facing uncertainty.
3. Develop Failure Resilience Training: Psychological research demonstrates that deliberately exposing ourselves to small failures while practicing constructive response patterns significantly enhances capacity for larger calculated risks.

27. Chasing money and status instead of meaningful, fulfilling work

This regret exemplifies what motivation researchers call "extrinsic goal dominance" – prioritizing external rewards over intrinsic satisfaction. The psychological foundation involves what social comparison theorists term "relative position sensitivity" – deriving self-worth from comparative advantage rather than intrinsic value creation.

This orientation often develops through what developmental psychologists identify as "contingent self-worth" – basing self-esteem on achievements rather than inherent value. Research by Richard Ryan and Edward Deci demonstrates that predominantly extrinsic motivation correlates with reduced well-being, creativity, and persistence compared to intrinsic motivation based on meaning, mastery, and autonomy.

The consequences manifest in what positive psychologists call "hedonic treadmill acceleration" – increased pursuit of external rewards (salary, status) to compensate for missing intrinsic satisfaction, creating a self-perpetuating cycle. Studies reveal that material success beyond moderate financial security contributes minimally to subjective well-being, while purpose and positive relationships demonstrate consistent, substantial impact.

Three evidence-based strategies for meaning-centered career focus:

1. Implement Job Crafting: Research shows that deliberately reshaping current roles to incorporate more strengths use, purpose orientation, and positive relationships significantly enhances meaning regardless of occupation.
2. Practice Contribution Orientation: Studies demonstrate that reframing work in terms of its positive impact on others rather than personal gain creates substantial increases in both meaning and satisfaction.
3. Develop Intrinsic Reward Sensitivity: Psychological research confirms that deliberately attending to internal markers of fulfillment (engagement, accomplishment, learning) rather than external validation enhances both satisfaction and performance quality.

28. Not starting the business or passion project I always dreamed of

This regret illustrates what entrepreneurship researchers call "implementation gap" – the disconnect between entrepreneurial intentions and corresponding actions. The psychological mechanism involves what uncertainty researchers term "ambiguity aversion" – our tendency to prefer known outcomes, even negative ones, over ambiguous possibilities.

This hesitation often reflects what mindset researchers identify as "fixed ability beliefs" – assuming talents and capabilities are largely static rather than expandable through effort. Studies by Carol Dweck demonstrate that individuals with growth mindsets show significantly greater willingness to embrace challenges and persist through setbacks – essential qualities for entrepreneurial success.

The consequences extend beyond unrealized ventures to identity formation. Research in developmental psychology reveals that creating something meaningful constitutes what Erik Erikson termed "generativity" – making a contribution that outlasts oneself, a crucial component of psychological well-being in middle and later adulthood. When entrepreneurial impulses remain unexpressed, individuals often experience what purpose researchers call "creative frustration" – a persistent sense of unexpressed potential.

Three evidence-based strategies for entrepreneurial activation:

1. Implement Minimum Viable Action: Research shows that identifying the smallest possible step toward a venture and executing it immediately dramatically reduces procrastination while providing critical feedback for refinement.
2. Practice Failure Normalization: Studies demonstrate that understanding setbacks as inevitable components of the entrepreneurial process rather than definitive judgments significantly increases persistence through challenges.
3. Develop Identity Scaffolding: Psychological research confirms that gradually incorporating entrepreneurial activities into self-concept through progressive commitment increases the likelihood of sustained action toward meaningful projects.

29. Remaining too long in a toxic or stressful work environment

This regret reflects what organizational psychologists call "maladaptive persistence" – remaining in harmful situations despite substantial personal costs. The psychological foundation involves what decision theorists term "escalation of commitment" – increasing investment in a chosen path despite mounting evidence it should be abandoned.

This persistence often stems from what cognitive psychologists identify as "sunk cost fallacy" – allowing prior investments to influence current decisions despite their irrelevance to future outcomes. Research demonstrates that toxic work environments create measurable physiological harm, including elevated inflammatory markers, compromised immune function, and increased cardiovascular risk – creating what health psychologists call "occupational stress disorder."

The consequences extend beyond immediate wellbeing to lasting personality changes. Studies show that prolonged exposure to negativity affects neural pathways, creating what neuroscientists term "negative affectivity bias" – increased sensitivity to threats and decreased capacity for positive engagement that persists even after environmental change. This often leads to what work-family researchers call "stress spillover" – transferring occupational distress to personal relationships.

Three evidence-based strategies for healthier workplace choices:

1. Implement Environmental Accounting: Research shows that systematically documenting both obvious and subtle costs of toxic environments (health impacts, relationship strain, emotional depletion) clarifies the true price of remaining.
2. Practice Psychological Detachment: Studies demonstrate that creating emotional distance through mindfulness techniques significantly reduces stress impacts while facilitating clearer decision-making about transitions.
3. Develop Support Network Activation: Psychological research confirms that deliberately cultivating resources outside the toxic environment (professional connections, financial reserves, emotional support) dramatically increases capacity to make necessary changes.

30. Not setting boundaries, allowing work to consume my life

This regret exemplifies what work-life researchers call "boundary permeability" – the progressive erosion of distinctions between professional and personal domains. The psychological mechanism involves what behavioral economists term "present bias" – systematically favoring immediate demands (responding to work email) over long-term benefits (relationship quality, personal renewal).

This pattern often reflects what identity researchers identify as "work-role centrality" – deriving disproportionate self-worth from professional identity while neglecting other life dimensions. Research demonstrates that continuous work availability activates stress response systems, preventing necessary recovery periods and creating what occupational health specialists call "allostatic overload" – physiological damage from chronic stress exposure.

The consequences extend beyond personal wellbeing to relationship quality. Studies reveal that technology-enabled work intrusions correlate with significant increases in family conflict and decreases in relationship satisfaction. Moreover, research in positive psychology demonstrates that activities outside work provide crucial dimensions of well-being – particularly relationships, personal interests, and community engagement – that remain undeveloped when work boundaries collapse.

Three evidence-based strategies for effective boundary management:

1. Implement Transition Rituals: Research shows that creating deliberate psychological shifts between work and personal roles (changing clothes, brief meditation, physical activity) enhances presence in both domains.

2. Practice Tech Containment: Studies demonstrate that establishing specific technology-free times and spaces significantly reduces work intrusions while enhancing recovery experiences.

3. Develop Values-Based Boundary Setting: Psychological research confirms that defining limits based on explicit values rather than external expectations dramatically increases both boundary maintenance and satisfaction with work-life integration.

31. Taking too few breaks or vacations, always being "on the job"

This regret illustrates what recovery researchers call "restoration deficit" – failing to provide necessary psychological and physiological replenishment between work periods. The psychological foundation involves what performance psychologists term "continuous productivity fallacy" – the mistaken belief that uninterrupted effort maximizes output, despite substantial evidence that strategic disengagement enhances both wellbeing and effectiveness.

This misconception often stems from what achievement researchers identify as "busywork valorization" – equating activity with accomplishment. Studies by organizational psychologist Sabine Sonnentag demonstrate that psychological detachment from work during non-work time significantly predicts both subjective wellbeing and objective performance, contradicting the "always on" approach to achievement.

The consequences manifest in what cognitive scientists call "attentional resource depletion" – diminished capacity for focus, creativity, and decision quality resulting from sustained directed attention without restoration. Beyond performance impacts, research shows that inadequate recreational time correlates with increased cardiovascular disease, depression, and overall mortality – creating what leisure researchers term "recovery debt" with cumulative health consequences.

Three evidence-based strategies for effective restoration:

1. Implement Strategic Recovery Periods: Research confirms that deliberate breaks throughout the workday (5-15 minutes every 90 minutes) significantly enhance both productivity and creativity compared to continuous effort.

2. Practice Full Engagement Vacations: Studies demonstrate that complete disconnection from work during scheduled time off provides crucial cognitive and emotional reset that improves life satisfaction and career sustainability.

3. Develop Microleisure Integration: Psychological research shows that incorporating brief pleasurable activities throughout daily routines creates cumulative restorative benefits that enhance overall wellbeing and work effectiveness.

32. Burning out by pushing myself too hard at work

This regret reflects what occupational health researchers call "self-endangering work behavior" – chronically exceeding personal capacity in pursuit of achievement. The psychological mechanism involves what motivation scientists term "performance-based self-esteem" – deriving self-worth primarily from professional accomplishments rather than intrinsic value.

This pattern often stems from what developmental psychologists identify as "unbalanced excellence orientation" – applying standards of exceptional performance across all domains without strategic selectivity. Research by burnout specialist Christina Maslach demonstrates that this approach creates vulnerability to the three dimensions of burnout: emotional exhaustion, cynicism, and reduced efficacy – a syndrome with profound implications for both wellbeing and performance.

The consequences extend beyond subjective distress to measurable physiological harm. Studies reveal that chronic overwork correlates with elevated inflammatory markers, hormonal dysregulation, and significant increases in serious health conditions including cardiovascular disease and depression. Moreover, burnout creates what career researchers call "vocational disillusionment" – diminished connection with work that once provided meaning and purpose, often leading to premature career abandonment.

Three evidence-based strategies for sustainable achievement:

1. Implement Energy Management: Research shows that attending to physical fundamentals (sleep, nutrition, exercise) and emotional wellbeing creates sustainable high performance compared to willpower-based approaches.

2. Practice Strategic Underachievement: Studies demonstrate that deliberately selecting areas for excellence versus adequacy dramatically reduces burnout risk while enhancing overall effectiveness.

3. Develop Meaning Anchors: Psychological research confirms that connecting work to personally significant values and impact provides motivational sustainability that outlasts achievement-based drives while protecting against burnout.

33. Not aligning my work with my values and passions

This regret exemplifies what positive psychologists call "values-vocation misalignment" – the persistent gap between one's authentic interests and daily work activities. The psychological mechanism involves what self-determination theory identifies as "intrinsic motivation deficit" – engaging primarily in activities driven by external rewards rather than inherent satisfaction.

Research demonstrates that work alignment with personal values significantly predicts what we call "eudaimonic well-being" – a sense of purpose, meaning, and self-actualization. In studies tracking thousands of individuals across careers, those whose work reflected their core values reported not only greater job satisfaction but also superior physical health markers, lower depression rates, and enhanced relationship quality compared to those experiencing value incongruence.

The consequences of sustained misalignment create what occupational psychologists term "identity fragmentation" – the psychological strain of projecting a professional self disconnected from one's authentic identity. This fragmentation requires emotional labor that depletes psychological resources, leading to what researchers call "authenticity exhaustion" – chronic depletion that affects all life domains.

Three evidence-based strategies for authentic vocational alignment:

1. Implement Values Clarification Exercise: Research demonstrates that systematically identifying your core values and assessing how current work expresses or violates them creates clarity that motivates meaningful change, even when constraints exist.
2. Practice Job Crafting: Studies show that deliberately reshaping elements of current roles to incorporate more personal values and strengths creates significant improvements in meaning and satisfaction without changing positions.
3. Develop Meaning Bridge Building: Psychological research confirms that actively connecting existing work to personally meaningful outcomes beyond immediate tasks substantially enhances purpose and well-being even in challenging environments.

34. Choosing my career based on others' expectations, not my own desires

This regret illustrates what developmental psychologists call "foreclosed identity" – committing to a career path without adequate exploration of personal interests and values. The psychological foundation involves what family systems theorists term "intergenerational transfer of unfulfilled aspirations" – parents consciously or unconsciously steering children toward careers that reflect parental values or unrealized dreams.

This pattern reflects a fundamental psychological tension between two core needs: autonomy (self-direction) and belonging (connection). Research demonstrates that when career choices primarily satisfy belonging needs at the expense of autonomy, individuals experience what motivation scientists call "controlled regulation" – pursuing goals without internal endorsement, which predicts lower persistence, creativity, and satisfaction compared to autonomous motivation.

The consequences manifest in what vocational psychologists identify as "authentic self atrophy" – the gradual diminishment of connection to personal interests and values when unexpressed professionally. Studies reveal that extended career misalignment correlates with elevated depression rates, psychosomatic symptoms, and identity crises, particularly during developmental transitions like midlife.

Three evidence-based strategies for reclaiming authentic career direction:

1. Implement Possible Selves Exploration: Research shows that systematically investigating alternative professional identities through structured reflection exercises activates autonomous motivation necessary for meaningful career recalibration.
2. Practice Psychological Differentiation: Studies demonstrate that deliberately separating self-worth from external validation substantially increases capacity to make authentic career choices despite potential disapproval.
3. Develop Incremental Alignment: Psychological research confirms that gradually introducing personally meaningful elements into current work before major transitions builds confidence while reducing resistance from both self and others.

35. Not using my talents and potential to the fullest in my work

This regret reflects what achievement psychologists call "capacity underutilization" – consistently performing below one's capabilities due to psychological barriers rather than ability limitations. The mechanism involves what mindset researchers identify as "fixed ability beliefs" – assuming talents are largely static qualities to be demonstrated rather than dynamic capacities to be developed.

This perspective creates what motivation scientists term "performance avoidance orientation" – focusing on preventing failure rather than achieving excellence. Research by Carol Dweck consistently demonstrates that this orientation leads to avoiding optimal challenges, reduced persistence after setbacks, and ultimately unrealized potential. The missed opportunity for "flow" experiences – that optimal state of complete engagement – represents a significant loss of both achievement and well-being.

The consequences extend beyond professional accomplishment to identity formation. Studies reveal that adults who consistently utilize their strengths report substantially higher levels of subjective well-being, self-efficacy, and meaning in life compared to those with similar abilities who don't exercise them. This suggests that talent utilization satisfies what positive psychologists call "competence need" – a foundational psychological requirement for human flourishing.

Three evidence-based strategies for talent fulfillment:

1. Implement Strengths-Based Focus: Research confirms that identifying signature strengths through validated assessments and deliberately creating opportunities to apply them significantly increases engagement and achievement.
2. Practice Growth Mindset Cultivation: Studies demonstrate that viewing abilities as developable through effort rather than fixed traits dramatically enhances willingness to embrace challenges that expand capabilities.
3. Develop Stretch Assignment Seeking: Psychological research shows that deliberately selecting projects slightly beyond current abilities creates optimal conditions for both skill development and increased confidence.

36. Letting fear of failure keep me stuck in a safe career

This regret exemplifies what clinical psychologists call "risk aversion syndrome" – allowing anxiety about potential negative outcomes to systematically override potential rewards. The psychological foundation involves what neuropsychologists term "threat vigilance bias" – our brain's evolutionary tendency to give greater weight to possible negative consequences than positive ones when facing uncertainty.

This protective mechanism creates what vocational psychologists identify as "career crystallization" – premature commitment to safe options before adequate exploration. Research demonstrates that this safety orientation correlates strongly with what we call "unmitigated agency" – pursuing security and control at the expense of growth and fulfillment, which studies consistently associate with diminished life satisfaction in later adulthood.

The consequences extend beyond missed opportunities to identity development. Studies reveal that moderate risk-taking in career contexts serves as what developmental psychologists call "identity catalyst" – accelerating self-discovery and personal growth in ways impossible through solely safe choices. When this catalyst remains inactive, individuals often experience what we term "self-concept stagnation" – diminished understanding of capabilities and interests.

Three evidence-based strategies for calibrated career risk-taking:

1. Implement Fear Decomposition Exercise: Research shows that systematically identifying and evaluating specific fears, rather than responding to generalized anxiety, dramatically improves decision quality under uncertainty.
2. Practice Failure Reframing: Studies demonstrate that conceptualizing setbacks as learning opportunities rather than character indictments significantly enhances willingness to pursue growth-oriented risks.
3. Develop Success-Independence Self-Worth: Psychological research confirms that deliberately separating identity from outcome dramatically reduces paralyzing perfectionism while increasing appropriate risk tolerance.

37. Not balancing work with leisure and family time (poor work-life balance)

This regret reflects what organizational psychologists call "work-role centrality dominance" – allowing professional identity to eclipse other life dimensions despite their importance to well-being. The psychological mechanism involves what behavioral economists term "present bias with domain neglect" – systematically prioritizing immediate work demands over equally important but less urgent personal domains.

This imbalance creates what positive psychologists identify as "dimensional atrophy" – the progressive weakening of capabilities and experiences in neglected life areas. Research confirms that well-being requires what we call "PERMA" development – Positive emotions, Engagement, Relationships, Meaning, and Accomplishment across multiple domains, not just work. Single-dimension investment inevitably produces diminishing returns compared to balanced development.

The consequences extend beyond subjective dissatisfaction to measurable health outcomes. Studies demonstrate that chronic work-life imbalance correlates with elevated inflammation markers, compromised immune function, and increased cardiovascular risk – creating what health psychologists term "allostatic overload" that accumulates across decades. Moreover, relationship research reveals that persistent imbalance predicts what family therapists call "functional absence" – being physically present but psychologically unavailable to loved ones.

Three evidence-based strategies for life domain balance:

1. Implement Time Portfolio Management: Research shows that deliberately allocating time across life dimensions proportionate to their importance significantly reduces value-behavior discrepancies and associated regret.
2. Practice Psychological Boundary Establishment: Studies demonstrate that creating clear delineations between work and personal domains through physical, temporal, and digital boundaries dramatically improves quality in both areas.
3. Develop Recovery Rhythm Implementation: Psychological research confirms that alternating periods of intensive work with deliberate renewal across multiple timeframes (daily, weekly, annually) optimizes both productivity and well-being.

38. Waiting too long to retire and enjoy life beyond work

This regret exemplifies what life-span psychologists call "third-act postponement" – delaying the transition to post-career activities until physical or cognitive capacities have diminished. The psychological foundation involves what identity researchers term "work-role entrenchment" –

excessive derivation of self-worth and purpose from professional identity, creating resistance to role transitions.

This resistance reflects what gerontologists identify as "continuity bias" – preferring familiar patterns despite changing personal needs and developmental stages. Research demonstrates that successful aging involves what we call "identity evolution" – the ability to develop new sources of meaning, contribution, and engagement appropriate to each life stage. When this evolution stalls due to rigid professional identification, individuals often experience what developmental psychologists term "generativity crisis" – difficulty finding purpose beyond career achievement.

The consequences extend beyond missed opportunities to health outcomes. Studies reveal that the sense of time limitation created by delayed retirement often generates what health psychologists call "compressed regret syndrome" – intensified distress over foreclosed possibilities combined with physical limitations that prevent full engagement in delayed activities. This creates substantial threats to well-being precisely when resources for psychological adaptation are diminishing.

Three evidence-based strategies for timely life transition:

1. Implement Possible Selves Exploration: Research shows that deliberately investigating post-career identities before retirement significantly enhances both transition readiness and subsequent satisfaction.
2. Practice Graduated Disengagement: Studies demonstrate that phased transitions through part-time work, consulting, or mentoring create psychological bridges that facilitate healthier adjustment than abrupt changes.
3. Develop Non-Work Identity Cultivation: Psychological research confirms that deliberately strengthening relationships, interests, and community involvements before retirement creates crucial identity resources that support well-being after career conclusion.

39. Not taking opportunities to learn new skills or grow in my career

This regret reflects what educational psychologists call "growth stagnation" – the premature plateau of skill development despite available learning opportunities. The psychological mechanism involves what mindset researchers identify as "comfort zone entrenchment" –

systematically avoiding experiences that create temporary incompetence necessary for new capability development.

This avoidance pattern stems from what cognitive psychologists term "performance-learning goal confusion" – prioritizing looking competent over becoming more competent. Research demonstrates that this orientation creates vulnerability to what motivation scientists call "skill obsolescence syndrome" – the gradual erosion of professional relevance and engagement when continuous learning is neglected.

The consequences extend beyond career implications to cognitive health. Studies reveal that intellectual challenge through ongoing learning serves as what neuroscientists identify as "cognitive reserve builder" – creating neural resources that protect against age-related cognitive decline. When learning opportunities are consistently avoided, individuals not only compromise professional trajectory but also accelerate cognitive aging processes.

Three evidence-based strategies for continuous growth:

1. Implement Learning Goal Orientation: Research shows that deliberately focusing on improvement rather than performance significantly increases willingness to embrace skill-building opportunities despite temporary discomfort.
2. Practice Deliberate Learning: Studies demonstrate that systematically identifying skill gaps and creating structured development plans dramatically enhances both capability acquisition and professional confidence.
3. Develop Growth Network Cultivation: Psychological research confirms that deliberately building relationships with individuals who exemplify continuous learning creates both practical support and motivational reinforcement for ongoing development.

40. Not leaving behind something meaningful through my work (a positive impact or legacy)

This regret exemplifies what existential psychologists call "contribution deficit" – the perception that one's work lacked meaningful impact beyond immediate tasks or personal gain. The psychological foundation involves what meaning researchers term "purpose-achievement gap" – successfully executing professional responsibilities without connecting them to broader significance.

This disconnection creates what positive psychologists identify as "meaning deficiency" – the absence of what humans fundamentally require for psychological flourishing. Research consistently demonstrates that perceived contribution to others' well-being serves as what we call a "eudaimonic amplifier" – dramatically enhancing subjective well-being beyond what personal achievement alone provides.

The consequences manifest in what developmental psychologists term "generativity crisis" – Erik Erikson's concept of the midlife struggle to create lasting positive impact. Studies reveal that individuals who perceive their work as primarily transactional rather than contributory report significantly higher rates of depression, existential anxiety, and regret intensity in later life stages compared to those who identified legitimate ways their work benefited others.

Three evidence-based strategies for meaningful contribution:

1. Implement Legacy Mapping Exercise: Research shows that systematically identifying how current work affects others now and potentially in the future significantly enhances perceived meaning regardless of occupation.
2. Practice Contribution Reframing: Studies demonstrate that deliberately reconceptualizing existing work through its impact on colleagues, customers, or community creates substantial increases in purpose experience.
3. Develop Mentoring Engagement: Psychological research confirms that deliberately investing in others' development creates what we call "vicarious achievement" – fulfillment through others' success that enhances legacy perception.

41. Not saving or planning financially for later life, leading to stress and limited options in my final years

This regret reflects what behavioral economists call "temporal discounting bias" – systematically undervaluing future needs compared to present desires. The psychological mechanism involves what neuroscientists identify as "present-self/future-self disconnection" – experiencing our future selves as fundamentally separate individuals whose welfare concerns us less than our present experience.

This cognitive bias creates what financial psychologists term "preparation avoidance" – postponing economic planning despite awareness of its importance. Research demonstrates that this avoidance often stems from what cognitive scientists call "complexity overwhelm" – the tendency to defer decisions perceived as requiring specialized knowledge or producing anxiety, even when delay creates substantially worse outcomes.

The consequences extend beyond financial limitations to psychological well-being. Studies reveal that financial insecurity in later life correlates strongly with elevated stress hormones, compromised immune function, and increased depression rates – creating what health researchers identify as "economic distress syndrome." Moreover, financial constraints often produce what autonomy theorists call "choice restriction" – the inability to select preferred living arrangements, healthcare options, or meaningful activities precisely when personal agency becomes increasingly important.

Three evidence-based strategies for financial preparation:

1. Implement Future-Self Visualization: Research shows that concretely imagining oneself in later life dramatically reduces present bias and increases willingness to allocate resources for future security.
2. Practice Automation Implementation: Studies demonstrate that establishing automatic savings systems that occur without active decision-making significantly improves long-term financial outcomes by bypassing psychological resistance.
3. Develop Financial Simplification: Psychological research confirms that creating straightforward, manageable planning approaches substantially increases implementation compared to complex optimal strategies that remain unexecuted.

Chapter 5. Personal Growth & Dreams

42. Not pursuing my passions and interests (outside of work or duties)

This regret exemplifies what positive psychologists call "engagement deficit syndrome" – the systematic underinvestment in activities that produce flow states, those optimal experiences characterized by complete absorption and intrinsic reward. The psychological mechanism involves what time-use researchers term "urgency bias" – consistently prioritizing tasks perceived as necessary over those experienced as nourishing.

This pattern creates what research identifies as "experiential impoverishment" – the gradual diminishment of positive emotion, meaning, and identity development that occurs when passion pursuits remain unexpressed. In studies tracking thousands of adults across decades, regular engagement with personal interests emerges as a significant predictor of psychological resilience, cognitive vitality, and subjective well-being, independent of socioeconomic factors.

The consequences extend beyond diminished pleasure to identity formation. Studies reveal that passion engagement serves as what developmental psychologists call "self-concordant activity" – behavior that expresses core aspects of personality, creating authenticity and integration. Without these expressions, individuals often experience what identity researchers term "core self atrophy" – a disconnection from defining aspects of personality that compromises psychological flourishing.

Three evidence-based strategies for passion integration:

1. Implement Micro-Passion Scheduling: Research shows that even brief, regular engagement with interests (15-30 minutes, 2-3 times weekly) produces significant well-being benefits while circumventing time-constraint barriers.
2. Practice Value Alignment: Studies demonstrate that connecting passion pursuits to core personal values substantially increases motivation and commitment even during busy periods.
3. Develop Social Accountability: Psychological research confirms that embedding interests within social structures (clubs, classes, partnerships) dramatically increases consistent engagement through commitment mechanisms and shared reinforcement.

43. Giving up on my dreams too early or never going after them at all

This regret reflects what goal psychologists call "premature disengagement" – abandoning aspirations before sufficient effort or in response to initial obstacles. The psychological foundation involves what cognitive scientists term "failure prediction error" – systematically overestimating the negative impact of setbacks while underestimating our remarkable capacity for resilience and adaptation.

This miscalculation creates what motivation researchers identify as "goal surrender" – relinquishing meaningful aspirations despite their continued personal significance. Studies reveal that abandoned dreams rarely disappear psychologically; instead, they persist as what narrative psychologists call "counterfactual identities" – alternative selves that remain psychologically active and become increasingly idealized over time, intensifying regret.

The consequences manifest in what researchers term the "aspiration-implementation gap" – the psychological discord created when internally valued goals remain unpursued. This discrepancy threatens what self-determination theorists identify as autonomy needs – our requirement to act in accordance with authentic values and interests – creating psychological distress that intensifies rather than diminishes with time.

Three evidence-based strategies for dream pursuit:

1. Implement Dream Decomposition: Research demonstrates that breaking aspirations into concrete, manageable steps significantly increases both initiation probability and persistence through obstacles.
2. Practice Failure Normalization: Studies show that understanding setbacks as inevitable components of any meaningful pursuit rather than signs of personal inadequacy dramatically enhances resilience and reduces premature disengagement.
3. Develop Implementation Intentions: Psychological research confirms that creating specific if-then plans ("If situation X occurs, I will do Y") increases goal-directed behavior by over 300% compared to mere goal setting.

44. Letting fear of failure keep me from trying new things and taking chances

This regret exemplifies what psychology terms "avoidance motivation dominance" – organizing behavior primarily around preventing negative outcomes rather than approaching positive possibilities. The psychological mechanism involves what neuroscientists identify as "negativity bias" – our brain's evolutionary tendency to give disproportionate weight to potential threats compared to rewards.

This protective orientation creates what developmental psychologists call "growth foreclosure" – systematically avoiding experiences that might produce temporary incompetence despite their growth potential. Research demonstrates that this foreclosure stems from what mindset theorists term "fixed ability beliefs" – viewing capabilities as static qualities rather than developable attributes, which predicts risk aversion and diminished resilience following setbacks.

The consequences extend beyond specific missed opportunities to personality development. Studies reveal that individuals who consistently choose safety over growth demonstrate significantly lower rates of psychological well-being, self-efficacy, and life satisfaction in later adulthood compared to those who periodically embrace challenge despite potential failure.

Three evidence-based strategies for overcoming failure fear:

1. Implement Growth Mindset Cultivation: Research shows that deliberately viewing abilities as developable rather than fixed qualities dramatically increases willingness to attempt challenging activities despite potential setbacks.
2. Practice "Failure Reframing": Studies demonstrate that conceptualizing failure as information rather than judgment creates a learning orientation that enhances subsequent performance and reduces avoidance.
3. Develop Courage Laddering: Psychological research confirms that gradually ascending through progressively challenging situations builds confidence and reduces fear through demonstrated success, making previously intimidating actions increasingly accessible.

45. Staying in my comfort zone and avoiding challenges or adventures

This regret illustrates what positive psychologists call "optimal arousal deprivation"—consistently choosing familiarity over the stimulating discomfort that catalyzes growth. The psychological foundation involves what behavioral scientists term "environmental habituation"—the diminishing psychological impact of familiar surroundings and experiences despite their initial satisfaction.

This habituation creates what motivation researchers identify as "novelty deficit" – insufficient variation in experience to maintain cognitive engagement and emotional vitality. Studies reveal that moderate, self-chosen discomfort serves as what neuropsychologists call "psychological cross-training" – creating mental flexibility, emotional resilience, and enhanced problem-solving capacity unavailable through comfortable routines.

The consequences manifest in what narrative psychologists term "story impoverishment" – the absence of meaningful challenges and their resolution in one's life narrative. Research demonstrates that individuals construct identity largely through challenge narratives, creating what Dan McAdams calls "redemptive sequences" – overcoming difficulty to discover strength. Without these sequences, life stories lack the rich complexity associated with psychological maturity and meaning.

Three evidence-based strategies for expanding comfort boundaries:

1. Implement Discomfort Scheduling: Research shows that deliberately planning regular, manageable challenges significantly enhances both psychological flexibility and subsequent satisfaction with routine experiences.
2. Practice Adventure Framing: Studies demonstrate that conceptualizing novel experiences as explorations rather than tests reduces anxiety while maintaining growth benefits, substantially increasing participation.
3. Develop Challenge Partnering: Psychological research confirms that facing new experiences with supportive companions dramatically reduces anticipatory anxiety while providing both accountability and shared enjoyment that reinforces future expansion.

46. Not traveling to the places or exploring the world as I had wished

This regret reflects what developmental psychologists call "experiential narrowing" – the progressive confinement of life experience to familiar geographical and cultural contexts despite opportunities for expansion. The psychological mechanism involves what decision scientists term "default bias" – our tendency to maintain current circumstances unless compelling reasons for change present themselves.

This inertia creates what cognitive psychologists identify as "perspective limitation" – restricted understanding stemming from insufficient exposure to diverse worldviews and lifestyles. Research demonstrates that meaningful travel serves as what cultural psychologists call "perspective-taking catalyst" – facilitating cognitive flexibility, tolerance for ambiguity, and cultural intelligence that transfer to multiple life domains beyond travel itself.

The consequences extend beyond missed pleasure to cognitive development. Studies reveal that immersion in unfamiliar cultural contexts activates neural pathways associated with creative problem-solving and cognitive flexibility, creating what neuroscientists term "mental model expansion" – the development of more sophisticated interpretive frameworks. Without these expansions, individuals often experience what meaning researchers call "frame stagnation" – increasingly rigid interpretations of experience.

Three evidence-based strategies for meaningful travel engagement:

1. Implement Destination Identification: Research shows that explicitly identifying personally significant locations dramatically increases both planning initiation and follow-through compared to vague travel aspirations.
2. Practice Experience Maximization: Studies demonstrate that allocating resources toward travel experiences rather than material acquisitions yields significantly greater and more enduring happiness returns.
3. Develop Cultural Immersion Orientation: Psychological research confirms that approaching travel as cultural engagement rather than mere sightseeing substantially enhances both enjoyment and lasting psychological impact.

47. Not having more adventures and memorable experiences in life

This regret exemplifies what positive psychologists call "peak experience deficiency" – insufficient engagement in activities that produce intense positive emotion, meaning, and memorability. The psychological foundation involves what economists term "present bias with future regret blindness" – systematically favoring immediate comfort over experiences that create enduring satisfaction and memory formation.

This trade-off creates what cognitive scientists identify as "autobiographical thinness" – insufficient standout experiences to create a rich, meaningful life narrative. Research demonstrates that autobiographical memory organizes around distinctive experiences rather than routine, with what memory researchers call "psychological punctuation marks" serving as critical reference points in our understanding of life progression and meaning.

The consequences manifest in what narrative psychologists term "story poverty" – the absence of vivid, emotionally significant episodes that provide narrative coherence and identity reinforcement. Studies reveal that individuals with experience-rich autobiographies report significantly higher levels of life satisfaction, meaning, and emotional complexity compared to those whose lives contain fewer distinctive experiences, despite similar objective circumstances.

Three evidence-based strategies for experience enrichment:

1. Implement Adventure Scheduling: Research shows that deliberately planning novel, challenging experiences creates both anticipatory pleasure and follow-through commitment that overcome inertia.
2. Practice Yes-First Policy: Studies demonstrate that adopting a default position of acceptance toward new opportunities (evaluating after rather than before experience) significantly increases participation in memorable activities.
3. Develop Experience Collection Mindset: Psychological research confirms that conceptualizing diverse experiences as valuable collectibles rather than mere activities enhances both motivation to participate and subsequent savoring.

48. Living according to others' expectations instead of being true to myself

This regret reflects what humanistic psychologists call "false-self living" – organizing behavior around external expectations rather than authentic values and interests. The psychological mechanism involves what developmental researchers term "contingent self-worth" – basing identity on others' approval rather than internal standards, creating vulnerability to social pressure and conformity.

This orientation stems from what attachment theorists identify as "conditional acceptance patterns" – early experiences suggesting that love and belonging depend on meeting others' expectations. Research demonstrates that this contingency creates what motivation scientists call "introjected regulation" – pursuing goals experienced as obligations rather than choices, which predicts diminished persistence, creativity, and fulfillment compared to autonomous motivation.

The consequences extend beyond specific choices to identity formation. Studies reveal that individuals who consistently prioritize external expectations over authentic inclinations report significantly higher rates of depression, anxiety, and identity crisis, particularly during life transitions when external guidance diminishes and personal direction becomes essential.

Three evidence-based strategies for authentic living:

1. Implement Values Clarification Exercise: Research shows that systematically identifying core personal values separate from internalized expectations creates clarity that facilitates autonomous decision-making.
2. Practice Authenticity Microskills: Studies demonstrate that beginning with small expressions of authentic preferences in lower-risk contexts gradually builds capacity for larger authenticity in more consequential domains.
3. Develop Supportive Authentication Network: Psychological research confirms that deliberately cultivating relationships with individuals who encourage authentic expression provides crucial reinforcement during challenging periods of self-alignment.

49. Caring too much about what others thought of me, rather than what I wanted

This regret exemplifies what social psychologists call "external validation dependency" – excessive reliance on others' approval for self-worth and decision validation. The psychological foundation involves what cognitive scientists term "spotlight effect" – systematically overestimating others' attention to and judgment of our actions and appearance.

This misperception creates what behavioral researchers identify as "impression management dominance" – organizing behavior primarily around creating favorable impressions rather than pursuing authentic interests. Research demonstrates that this orientation correlates with what personality psychologists call "social reactivity" – heightened sensitivity to rejection and criticism that further reinforces approval-seeking behavior, creating a self-perpetuating cycle.

The consequences manifest in what existential psychologists term "agency surrender" – relinquishing authorship of one's life to an imagined external audience. Studies reveal that individuals with strong internal validation orientations report significantly higher levels of life satisfaction, resilience after setbacks, and authentic self-expression compared to those primarily motivated by external validation, despite similar objective circumstances.

Three evidence-based strategies for internal validation development:

1. Implement Audience Delusion Reduction: Research shows that recognizing others' attention is typically brief and significantly less evaluative than assumed dramatically reduces approval-seeking behavior.

2. Practice Value-Guided Decision Making: Studies demonstrate that explicitly evaluating choices against personal values rather than anticipated social reaction substantially increases both decision satisfaction and psychological well-being.

3. Develop Rejection Resilience: Psychological research confirms that gradually expanding comfort with potential disapproval through progressive exposure significantly reduces approval dependency while enhancing authentic expression.

50. Not developing or using my creative talents (writing, art, music, etc.)

This regret reflects what creativity researchers call "creative expression suppression" – the systematic inhibition of artistic impulses despite their psychological importance. The mechanism involves what motivation scientists term "creativity threat response" – anxiety triggered by the vulnerability inherent in creative expression, particularly fear of judgment, inadequacy, or wasted effort.

This anxiety creates what developmental psychologists identify as "creative foreclosure" – abandoning artistic pursuits before sufficient exploration and development. Research demonstrates that creative expression serves as what positive psychologists call "flow catalyst" – facilitating optimal experiences characterized by complete engagement and intrinsic reward that contribute significantly to psychological well-being.

The consequences extend beyond diminished pleasure to identity restriction. Studies reveal that creative activities function as what self-determination theorists call "competence satisfaction vehicles" – providing experiences of mastery and growth that fulfill fundamental psychological needs. Without these expressions, individuals often experience what purpose researchers term "contribution limitation" – restricted outlets for meaningful personal contribution.

Three evidence-based strategies for creative engagement:

1. Implement Process Orientation: Research shows that focusing on creative experience rather than outcomes significantly reduces performance anxiety while enhancing both engagement quality and persistence.

2. Practice Creativity Microcommitments: Studies demonstrate that scheduling brief, regular creative sessions (15-30 minutes) dramatically increases both consistency and development compared to occasional longer periods.

3. Develop Judgment Suspension Techniques: Psychological research confirms that deliberately separating creation from evaluation phases substantially enhances creative output and satisfaction by circumventing self-criticism that typically inhibits expression.

51. Not dedicating time to continuous learning and personal growth

This regret exemplifies what cognitive psychologists call "intellectual stagnation" – the cessation of deliberate learning despite cognitive capacity for continued development. The psychological foundation involves what behavioral economists term "knowledge investment myopia" – systematically undervaluing future benefits of current learning efforts while overvaluing immediate convenience.

This miscalculation creates what neuropsychologists identify as "cognitive reserve deficit" – insufficient mental stimulation to maintain neural plasticity and cognitive flexibility. Research demonstrates that continued intellectual engagement serves as what gerontologists call "cognitive protection" – building resilience against age-related decline through enhanced neural connectivity and processing efficiency.

The consequences extend beyond cognitive health to existential well-being. Studies reveal that ongoing learning satisfies what motivation researchers term "growth needs" – psychological requirements for continued development and mastery that remain active throughout adulthood. Without fulfillment of these needs, individuals often experience what meaning theorists call "stagnation distress" – the uncomfortable awareness of developmental potential remaining unrealized.

Three evidence-based strategies for lifelong learning:

1. **Implement Learning Integration**: Research shows that incorporating learning into existing routines through audiobooks, podcasts, or brief reading sessions dramatically increases consistency compared to separate learning activities.

2. **Practice Interest-Based Learning Selection**: Studies demonstrate that pursuing knowledge in areas of genuine curiosity creates substantially greater engagement and retention than obligation-driven learning.

3. **Develop Learning Community Engagement**: Psychological research confirms that participating in groups focused on knowledge acquisition (book clubs, courses, discussion groups) significantly enhances both commitment and enjoyment through social reinforcement.

52. Wasting too much time on trivial matters instead of enriching my mind

This regret reflects what attention researchers call "engagement misallocation" – investing disproportionate cognitive resources in activities with minimal developmental or satisfaction return. The psychological mechanism involves what behavioral scientists term "path of least resistance decision-making" – defaulting to immediately accessible, low-effort activities despite their limited value.

This tendency creates what positive psychologists identify as "flow opportunity cost" – displacing potentially engaging, meaningful experiences with passive consumption that neither challenges nor fulfills. Research demonstrates that activities requiring active cognitive engagement produce what neuroscientists call "productive cognitive stress" – optimal mental challenge that enhances neural connectivity and psychological development.

The consequences manifest in what time-use researchers term "retrospective time poverty" – the perception when reflecting on past periods that time was abundant but poorly utilized. Studies reveal that individuals who regularly engage in cognitively active pursuits report significantly higher levels of life satisfaction, purpose, and psychological complexity compared to those primarily engaged in passive consumption, regardless of total leisure time available.

Three evidence-based strategies for meaningful engagement:

1. Implement Activity Value Assessment: Research shows that periodically evaluating how specific activities contribute to well-being, growth, or meaning significantly improves time allocation decisions.
2. Practice Intentional Consumption: Studies demonstrate that deliberately selecting media and activities aligned with personal development goals rather than defaulting to whatever's available substantially enhances both enjoyment and benefit.
3. Develop High-Value Accessibility: Psychological research confirms that deliberately structuring environments to make enriching activities more immediately accessible than

trivial alternatives dramatically shifts behavior patterns without requiring continuous willpower.

53. Not discovering or pursuing a clear purpose in life

This regret exemplifies what positive psychologists call "purpose deficit syndrome" – navigating life without an organizing principle that provides direction and meaning. The psychological foundation involves what existential theorists term "teleological vacuum" – the absence of a perceived aim toward which one's efforts are directed, creating a fragmented rather than integrated sense of life.

Research on purpose demonstrates its profound impact on wellbeing. In studies, individuals with a clear sense of purpose show significantly greater longevity, reduced incidence of Alzheimer's disease, and superior cardiovascular health compared to those without such direction. Purpose functions as what psychologists call an "existential immune system" – providing resilience during inevitable life challenges by contextualizing difficulties within a broader meaningful framework.

The consequences of purpose absence create what meaning researchers identify as "existential drift" – the sense of moving through life responding to circumstances rather than pursuing a personally significant direction. Studies reveal that purpose fulfills our fundamental need for coherence – the psychological requirement that our actions connect to values and goals larger than immediate gratification.

Three evidence-based strategies for purpose development:

1. Implement Contribution Mapping: Research shows that systematically identifying where your strengths and interests intersect with others' needs creates natural purpose pathways by connecting personal fulfillment with meaningful impact.
2. Practice Values Clarification: Studies demonstrate that explicitly articulating core values and evaluating activities against them significantly enhances purpose development by revealing consistent themes across seemingly disparate interests.
3. Develop Legacy Perspective: Psychological research confirms that considering what you hope to have contributed by life's end creates motivational clarity that organizes present decisions around enduring rather than transient concerns.

54. Not taking time for self-reflection and understanding myself sooner

This regret reflects what developmental psychologists call "self-knowledge deficit" – insufficient understanding of one's authentic needs, values, and patterns. The psychological mechanism involves what cognition researchers term "introspective avoidance" – the tendency to focus attention outward rather than inward, despite the crucial role self-understanding plays in effective decision-making.

This avoidance creates what identity theorists identify as "unexamined living" – making choices based on unquestioned assumptions, social defaults, or immediate impulses rather than consciously held values. Research demonstrates that self-awareness serves as what metacognitive psychologists call "decision calibration" – aligning choices with authentic preferences rather than transient influences.

The consequences extend beyond suboptimal decisions to identity development. Studies reveal that individuals with greater self-knowledge demonstrate significantly higher levels of well-being, relationship satisfaction, and career fulfillment compared to those lacking such insight. The psychological mechanism appears to involve what researchers call "choice-self congruence" – the alignment between decisions and authentic preferences that creates subjective authenticity.

Three evidence-based strategies for self-knowledge development:

1. Implement Structured Reflection Practice: Research shows that regular journaling with specific prompts about emotions, patterns, and values significantly enhances self-awareness compared to unstructured reflection or external focus.
2. Practice Feedback Integration: Studies demonstrate that deliberately soliciting and processing input from trusted others provides crucial perspective on blind spots inaccessible through introspection alone.
3. Develop Decision Review Protocols: Psychological research confirms that systematically examining past choices for patterns and outcomes creates accelerated learning about preferences and tendencies that would otherwise require decades to discern.

55. Not building the self-confidence to pursue what truly mattered to me

This regret exemplifies what cognitive psychologists call "self-efficacy deficiency" – insufficient belief in one's capacity to effectively navigate challenges or achieve meaningful goals. The psychological foundation involves what attributional theorists term "negative competence assessment" – systematically underestimating abilities while overestimating obstacles.

This assessment creates what behavioral scientists identify as "preemptive disengagement" – avoiding pursuits despite their importance due to anticipated failure rather than actual incapacity. Research demonstrates that self-confidence functions as what motivational psychologists call "psychological activation energy" – the initial belief necessary to begin challenging pursuits that subsequently generate their own momentum through progressive success.

The consequences manifest in what developmental researchers term "potential-achievement gap" – the distance between capacity and actual accomplishment attributable to psychological rather than ability limitations. Studies reveal that perceived self-efficacy predicts achievement across domains more reliably than objective ability measures, suggesting confidence affects outcome largely through its impact on effort, persistence, and challenge-seeking.

Three evidence-based strategies for confidence development:

1. Implement Graduated Success Sequencing: Research shows that structuring challenges in progressive difficulty creates confidence through accumulated evidence of capability that transfers to larger pursuits.
2. Practice Self-Talk Reconstruction: Studies demonstrate that deliberately replacing self-limiting narratives with accurate, constructive interpretations significantly enhances performance through reduced anxiety and increased effort.
3. Develop Competence Documentation: Psychological research confirms that maintaining records of capabilities, skills, and past successes creates objective evidence that counters subjective insecurity during challenging situations.

56. Hesitating and missing opportunities that could have changed my life

This regret reflects what decision scientists call "temporal opportunity neglect" – failing to recognize and act upon time-limited possibilities despite their potential value. The psychological mechanism involves what behavioral economists term "status quo bias" – our tendency to maintain current circumstances despite superior alternatives due to loss aversion and uncertainty avoidance.

This bias creates what opportunity researchers identify as "decision paralysis" – overthinking choices until the window for action closes. Research demonstrates that meaningful opportunities often have what game theorists call "temporal scarcity" – limited availability that requires relatively quick response rather than extended deliberation. This temporal constraint conflicts with our evolved tendency toward caution when facing uncertainty.

The consequences extend beyond specific missed chances to identity formation. Studies reveal that individuals who periodically embrace significant opportunities report greater life satisfaction, personal growth, and narrative richness compared to those who consistently prioritize stability. The psychological mechanism appears to involve what developmental researchers call "identity elasticity" – the capacity to incorporate new possibilities into self-concept rather than rejecting them as threatening.

Three evidence-based strategies for opportunity engagement:

1. Implement Regret Minimization Framework: Research shows that evaluating opportunities through the lens of future regret ("Will I wish I had taken this chance?") significantly enhances decision quality during temporal constraints.
2. Practice Opportunity Triage: Studies demonstrate that developing clear, personal criteria for quickly evaluating opportunities creates capacity for timely response without sacrificing decision quality.
3. Develop Decision Efficiency: Psychological research confirms that deliberately reducing deliberation time for moderate-stakes decisions preserves resources for truly consequential choices while preventing paralysis for time-sensitive opportunities.

57. Taking life too seriously and not allowing myself to have more fun

This regret exemplifies what positive psychologists call "positive affect deficit" – insufficient experience of joy, playfulness, and lightheartedness despite their contribution to psychological well-being. The psychological foundation involves what cognitive theorists term "responsibility dominance" – overemphasizing obligation and seriousness at the expense of pleasure and enjoyment.

This imbalance creates what emotion researchers identify as "hedonic suppression" – habitually restricting positive emotion expression due to internalized beliefs about propriety, productivity, or maturity. Research demonstrates that positive emotions serve as what neuropsychologists call "psychological broadening agents" – expanding cognitive flexibility, creativity, and social connection in ways that enhance both immediate experience and long-term resilience.

The consequences extend beyond diminished pleasure to cognitive functioning. Studies reveal that individuals with greater positive emotion experience demonstrate enhanced problem-solving ability, superior stress recovery, and more effective immune function compared to those with predominantly serious orientation. The biological mechanism appears to involve what researchers call "physiological undoing" – positive emotions' capacity to counteract stress response activation.

Three evidence-based strategies for enhancing positive engagement:

1. Implement Play Scheduling: Research shows that deliberately allocating time for enjoyable activities without practical purpose significantly increases wellbeing through both anticipatory pleasure and experienced joy.
2. Practice Positive Reinterpretation: Studies demonstrate that finding humorous or lighthearted perspectives on stressful situations creates psychological distance and emotional regulation unavailable through serious focus alone.
3. Develop Permission Structures: Psychological research confirms that explicitly creating contexts where playfulness is validated substantially reduces self-consciousness that often inhibits enjoyment, particularly for those with strong responsibility orientation.

58. Not trying hobbies or activities I was curious about

This regret reflects what motivation researchers call "exploration deficit" – insufficient engagement with novel activities despite their contribution to personal development and well-being. The psychological mechanism involves what decision theorists term "inertial decision-making" – defaulting to familiar patterns despite curiosity about alternatives due to activation energy required for new pursuits.

This inertia creates what developmental psychologists identify as "interest atrophy" – the gradual narrowing of activities and engagement that often accompanies aging despite continued capacity for new interests. Research demonstrates that novel activity engagement serves as what neuroscientists call "cognitive enrichment" – creating new neural connections that enhance mental flexibility and protect against cognitive decline.

The consequences extend beyond missed enjoyment to identity limitation. Studies reveal that individuals who regularly explore new interests demonstrate greater psychological complexity, creative problem-solving, and subjective vitality compared to those with static activity patterns. The psychological mechanism appears to involve what researchers call "self-expansion" – incorporating new capabilities and experiences into identity in ways that enhance both self-concept and wellbeing.

Three evidence-based strategies for exploration enhancement:

1. Implement Curiosity Tracking: Research shows that maintaining a simple record of activities that spark interest significantly increases follow-through compared to relying on memory alone.
2. Practice Microtrial Experimentation: Studies demonstrate that sampling new activities through minimal initial commitments (single classes, borrowed equipment) substantially reduces barriers to exploration while providing sufficient information for interest assessment.
3. Develop Interest Communities: Psychological research confirms that exploring new activities within supportive social contexts dramatically increases both initial comfort and sustained engagement through shared learning and mutual encouragement.

59. Never taking the leap to live in a different city or country when I had the chance

This regret exemplifies what cultural psychologists call "environmental stagnation" – remaining in familiar geographical and cultural contexts despite opportunities for expansion. The psychological foundation involves what decision scientists term "ambiguity aversion" – our preference for known circumstances despite their limitations over novel environments with uncertain outcomes.

This aversion creates what developmental researchers identify as "perspective confinement" – limited understanding stemming from insufficient exposure to diverse worldviews, values, and lifestyles. Research demonstrates that geographical relocation serves as what cognitive scientists call "frame disruption" – challenging implicit assumptions about normality by revealing alternative ways of living that remain invisible within culturally homogeneous environments.

The consequences manifest in what identity theorists term "experiential narrowing" — constricted self-knowledge resulting from limited environmental variation. Studies reveal that individuals who experience meaningful cultural immersion demonstrate enhanced cognitive flexibility, cultural intelligence, and tolerance for ambiguity compared to those who remain in familiar contexts throughout life.

Three evidence-based strategies for geographical exploration:

1. Implement Location Experimentation: Research shows that extended visits (3-6 weeks) to potential relocation destinations provide crucial data for evaluation while minimizing commitment risk associated with permanent moves.
2. Practice Incremental Expansion: Studies demonstrate that beginning with locations moderately different from familiar environments before attempting radical changes significantly increases adjustment success and psychological benefit.
3. Develop Reintegration Planning: Psychological research confirms that deliberately incorporating valued elements of new locations into permanent lifestyle dramatically enhances long-term impact even when temporary immersion is the only feasible option.

60. Not standing up for myself or setting healthy boundaries with others

This regret reflects what interpersonal psychologists call "boundary deficit disorder" — insufficient protection of personal needs, values, and resources in relationships. The psychological mechanism involves what social scientists term "approval dependency" — prioritizing others' validation over personal wellbeing due to fear of rejection or conflict.

This dependency creates what clinical psychologists identify as "compromised agency" — diminished capacity to act according to authentic preferences when they conflict with others' expectations. Research demonstrates that healthy boundaries serve as what relational theorists call "psychological infrastructure" — creating sustainable relationships by balancing connection with appropriate separation.

The consequences extend beyond relationship dynamics to identity formation. Studies reveal that individuals with effective boundary maintenance demonstrate significantly higher levels of self-respect, authentic expression, and relational satisfaction compared to those with insufficient limits. The psychological mechanism appears to involve what researchers call "self-integrity preservation" — maintaining core values and needs despite external pressure.

Three evidence-based strategies for boundary development:

1. Implement Value-Based Boundary Setting: Research shows that establishing limits based on explicitly identified personal values rather than reactions to others' behavior significantly enhances consistency and reduces guilt.

2. Practice Graduated Assertion: Studies demonstrate that beginning with lower-risk boundary enforcement before attempting higher-stakes situations substantially increases success through progressive skill development.

3. Develop Discomfort Tolerance: Psychological research confirms that deliberately expanding capacity to withstand others' negative reactions dramatically improves boundary maintenance, as enforcement difficulty typically stems from emotional discomfort rather than skill deficits.

61. Ignoring my intuition and inner voice in making life decisions

This regret exemplifies what decision scientists call "intuitive intelligence neglect" – discounting internal knowing despite its valuable contribution to effective choice-making. The psychological foundation involves what cognitive researchers term "analytical dominance" – overvaluing explicit reasoning while undervaluing intuitive processing despite the latter's superior capacity for integrating complex information patterns.

This imbalance creates what neuroscientists identify as "somatic marker suppression" – ignoring bodily signals that reflect unconscious pattern recognition accumulated through experience. Research demonstrates that effective decision-making integrates what dual-process theorists call "System 1" (rapid, intuitive) and "System 2" (deliberate, analytical) thinking rather than relying exclusively on either approach.

The consequences manifest in what decision quality researchers term "alignment failure" – choices that satisfy explicit criteria but violate deeper values or needs identified through intuitive processes. Studies reveal that individuals who integrate intuition with analysis report greater decision satisfaction, reduced regret intensity, and superior outcomes compared to those employing predominantly analytical approaches.

Three evidence-based strategies for intuitive integration:

1. Implement Somatic Awareness Practice: Research shows that deliberately attending to bodily responses during decision-making significantly enhances access to intuitive information typically processed below conscious awareness.

2. Practice Intuitive Journaling: Studies demonstrate that recording initial impressions before analytical consideration preserves intuitive insights that often become inaccessible during subsequent deliberation.

3. Develop Decision Quieting: Psychological research confirms that creating periods of mental stillness through meditation or similar practices substantially improves intuitive signal detection by reducing cognitive noise that typically obscures subtle internal knowing.

Chapter 6. Health & Well-Being

62. Neglecting my health and self-care over the years

This regret exemplifies what health psychologists call "temporal health discounting" — systematically undervaluing future well-being compared to present convenience. The psychological mechanism involves what behavioral economists term "present bias" — our tendency to disproportionately weight immediate rewards over long-term benefits despite their objective importance.

This bias creates what preventive health researchers identify as the "prevention paradox" — the challenge that health-protective behaviors require consistent investment with delayed and often invisible returns. Research demonstrates that our cognitive architecture evolved to respond to immediate threats rather than gradual risks, creating a fundamental mismatch with modern health challenges that develop incrementally over decades.

The consequences manifest in what gerontologists call "compressed morbidity reversal" — the tragic condensing of active, healthy years that could have extended throughout later life. Studies reveal that individuals who consistently prioritize health habits demonstrate an average of 12-14 additional years of high-quality life compared to those who neglect basic self-care.

Three evidence-based strategies for proactive health integration:

1. Implement Health Investment Reframing: Research shows that conceptualizing health behaviors as immediate gains (enhanced energy, mood improvement, better sleep) rather than distant protection dramatically increases adherence by leveraging our present-focus tendency.

2. Practice Environmental Pre-commitment: Studies demonstrate that deliberately structuring your surroundings to facilitate healthy choices (keeping running shoes visible, preparing nutritious meals in advance) significantly enhances consistency by reducing decision points.

3. Develop Small Habits Integration: Psychological research confirms that embedding modest health behaviors within existing routines creates sustainable patterns that accumulate into significant impacts without requiring major lifestyle disruption.

63. Not eating a healthy diet or paying attention to nutrition

This regret reflects what nutritional psychologists call "dietary mindfulness deficit" – consuming food based predominantly on immediate taste, convenience, or emotional comfort rather than nutritional value. The psychological foundation involves what neuroscientists term "reward sensitivity overriding" – high-calorie, low-nutrient foods triggering dopamine pathways that evolved when caloric scarcity, not abundance, was our primary dietary challenge.

This override creates what metabolic researchers identify as "nutritional mismatch syndrome" – the progressive deterioration of biological function when modern eating patterns conflict with our evolved nutritional needs. Research demonstrates that diet quality serves as what epidemiologists call a "fundamental health determinant" – influencing virtually every body system and predicting disease risk more powerfully than many genetic factors.

The consequences extend beyond specific illnesses to quality of life. Studies reveal that dietary patterns significantly predict cognitive function, emotional well-being, and energy levels independent of weight or disease status – creating what nutritional scientists term "sub-clinical nutritional impact" that affects daily functioning long before diagnosable conditions develop.

Three evidence-based strategies for nutritional enhancement:

1. Implement Addition Before Subtraction: Research shows that focusing initially on incorporating nutritious foods rather than eliminating problematic ones creates sustainable dietary improvement through positive reinforcement rather than restriction.
2. Practice Environmental Nutrition Design: Studies demonstrate that deliberately structuring food environments (visible fruit, prepared vegetables, pre-portioned treats) dramatically improves nutritional choices by reducing decision fatigue.
3. Develop Eating Awareness: Psychological research confirms that mindful attention to hunger signals, satisfaction cues, and emotional triggers substantially enhances both nutritional quality and eating enjoyment by interrupting automatic consumption patterns.

64. Not staying physically active with regular exercise

This regret exemplifies what exercise physiologists call "movement deprivation syndrome" – the progressive deterioration of physical capacity resulting from insufficient activity despite our biological design for regular movement. The psychological mechanism involves what motivational scientists term "effort-reward miscalculation" – overestimating the discomfort of exercise while underestimating its substantial psychological and physical benefits.

This miscalculation creates what health researchers identify as "activity threshold avoidance" – the tendency to perceive exercise as requiring more time, intensity, or structure than is actually necessary for significant health benefits. Research demonstrates that even modest activity – 20-30 minutes of walking daily – reduces mortality risk by approximately 30%, yet this threshold seems insufficiently impressive to motivate consistent action.

The consequences extend beyond physical health to psychological functioning. Studies reveal that regular physical activity serves as what psychiatric researchers call "broad-spectrum intervention" – demonstrating effectiveness comparable to medication for mild to moderate depression and anxiety while simultaneously enhancing cognitive function, sleep quality, and stress resilience.

Three evidence-based strategies for sustainable activity:

1. **Implement Movement Snacking**: Research shows that accumulating brief activity periods throughout the day (3-10 minute "movement snacks") provides comparable benefits to longer sessions while dramatically reducing perceived barriers.

2. **Practice Enjoyment Matching**: Studies demonstrate that selecting activities based primarily on pleasure rather than caloric expenditure or intensity increases consistency by over 300% over long-term periods.

3. **Develop Identity-Based Movement**: Psychological research confirms that conceptualizing exercise as an expression of personal identity ("I'm someone who enjoys moving") rather than an external obligation creates intrinsic motivation that sustains behavior through inevitable obstacles.

65. Abusing my body with harmful substances (e.g., smoking, excessive alcohol, drugs)

This regret reflects what addiction researchers call "toxic reward substitution" – seeking temporary neurochemical relief through substances that ultimately compromise the brain's natural reward capacity. The psychological foundation involves what stress-response theorists term "maladaptive coping mechanism" – utilizing substances to manage emotional or social challenges despite their long-term consequences.

This mechanism creates what neuroscientists identify as "hedonic regulation dysregulation" – progressive impairment of the brain's ability to experience natural pleasure as substance use modifies reward pathways. Research demonstrates that many substance dependencies begin as rational attempts to address legitimate needs (stress relief, social connection, emotional regulation) before transforming into compulsions that compromise rather than enhance functioning.

The consequences extend beyond health impacts to relational and identity dimensions. Studies reveal that substance dependence progressively narrows behavioral repertoire around acquisition and use, creating what addiction specialists call "purpose displacement" – the gradual substitution of substance-related activities for previously meaningful pursuits and connections.

Three evidence-based strategies for substance management:

1. Implement Needs Identification: Research shows that explicitly identifying the legitimate needs substances currently address (stress relief, social connection, emotional regulation) significantly enhances success by enabling development of healthier alternatives.
2. Practice Environmental Restructuring: Studies demonstrate that deliberately modifying contexts associated with substance use dramatically reduces consumption by interrupting automatic behavioral sequences.
3. Develop Meaningful Engagement Alternatives: Psychological research confirms that cultivating activities that provide purpose, mastery, and connection creates natural reward experiences that compete effectively with substance-induced states.

66. Ignoring health warning signs and delaying medical checkups

This regret exemplifies what medical psychologists call "health vigilance avoidance" – deliberately disregarding potential indicators of medical issues despite their potential significance. The psychological mechanism involves what cognitive scientists term "information aversion" – our tendency to avoid data that might require uncomfortable actions or generate anxiety, even when such avoidance increases objective risk.

This aversion creates what preventive health researchers identify as "detection lag" – the crucial time period between when a condition becomes detectable and when it is actually diagnosed, often making the difference between straightforward treatment and complex intervention. Research demonstrates that this delay reflects not merely negligence but active avoidance that serves immediate emotional regulation at the expense of long-term welfare.

The consequences manifest in what oncologists call "stage migration" – the progression of potentially manageable conditions into more serious states that require more invasive treatment with poorer outcomes. Studies reveal that simple screening procedures significantly reduce mortality for numerous conditions including colorectal, breast, cervical, and skin cancers – making avoidance particularly consequential.

Three evidence-based strategies for appropriate health vigilance:

1. Implement Fear Compartmentalization: Research shows that deliberately separating the process of information gathering from treatment decisions significantly increases screening participation by reducing anticipated anxiety.
2. Practice Scheduling Precommitment: Studies demonstrate that establishing automatic appointment systems (annual physicals, recommended screenings) dramatically increases follow-through by eliminating repeated decision points.
3. Develop Medical Partnership Orientation: Psychological research confirms that conceptualizing medical professionals as collaborators rather than authority figures substantially improves both information seeking and adherence to recommendations.

67. Waiting too long to see a doctor, so problems worsened

This regret reflects what medical decision theorists call "treatment procrastination" – delaying necessary medical intervention despite awareness of concerning symptoms. The psychological foundation involves what cognitive scientists term "uncertainty aversion" – our tendency to postpone action when outcomes are ambiguous, despite evidence that delay often increases uncertainty rather than resolving it.

This aversion creates what health psychologists identify as the "reassurance-seeking paradox" – postponing medical consultation while simultaneously seeking confirmation that symptoms aren't serious, often through inadequate sources like internet searches or non-expert opinions.

Research demonstrates that this pattern serves short-term anxiety management while potentially compromising long-term health outcomes.

The consequences manifest in what medical economists call "treatment escalation" – the increased intervention intensity, cost, and side-effect burden resulting from addressing conditions at advanced rather than early stages. Studies reveal that delayed treatment not only affects physical outcomes but creates what health psychologists term "retrospective responsibility distress" – the particularly painful awareness that suffering was partially self-initiated through postponement.

Three evidence-based strategies for timely medical engagement:

1. Implement Symptom Documentation Protocol: Research shows that systematically recording concerning symptoms with specific parameters (duration, intensity, impact) provides objective data that counteracts subjective minimization.
2. Practice Advance Decision Formulation: Studies demonstrate that pre-determining what symptom thresholds will trigger medical consultation significantly increases appropriate action by removing in-the-moment decision-making.
3. Develop Health Advocacy Mindset: Psychological research confirms that conceptualizing medical attention as a form of self-advocacy rather than weakness or overreaction substantially improves timely care-seeking behavior.

68. Allowing stress to dominate my life and not managing it properly

This regret exemplifies what stress researchers call "allostatic overload syndrome" – the cumulative biological and psychological damage resulting from chronic, unmanaged stress activation. The psychological mechanism involves what neuroscientists term "threat vigilance dominance" – excessive activation of neural circuits evolved for responding to immediate physical dangers rather than contemporary psychological challenges.

This dominance creates what psychoneuroimmunologists identify as "physiological wear patterns" – the gradual deterioration of cardiovascular, immune, digestive, and neurological systems under persistent stress hormones. Research demonstrates that unmanaged stress functions as what epidemiologists call a "meta-risk factor" – amplifying vulnerability across virtually all disease categories through both direct physiological effects and indirect behavioral impacts.

The consequences extend beyond physical health to experiential quality. Studies reveal that chronic stress creates what consciousness researchers call "present-moment extraction" – the diminished capacity to fully engage with current experience due to persistent anticipatory anxiety or rumination. This extraction progressively erodes life satisfaction regardless of objective circumstances.

Three evidence-based strategies for effective stress regulation:

1. Implement Stress Response Differentiation: Research shows that distinguishing between productive stress (motivating action) and unproductive rumination significantly improves management by targeting interventions appropriately.
2. Practice Physiological Reset Activities: Studies demonstrate that brief but regular stress-countering practices (diaphragmatic breathing, progressive relaxation, guided imagery) create measurable biological recovery that prevents accumulation effects.
3. Develop Control Boundary Clarification: Psychological research confirms that explicitly distinguishing between circumstances within and beyond personal control substantially reduces stress reactivity by focusing attention on constructive response options.

69. Not prioritizing rest and sleep for my well-being

This regret reflects what sleep researchers call "restorative deficit disorder" – chronic insufficient recovery time despite its fundamental necessity for biological and psychological functioning. The psychological foundation involves what performance psychologists term "productivity-recovery imbalance" – overvaluing continuous activity while undervaluing essential restoration periods.

This imbalance creates what neuroscientists identify as "cognitive resource depletion" – the progressive deterioration of attention, decision quality, emotional regulation, and creativity resulting from inadequate renewal. Research demonstrates that consistent sleep restriction (less than 7 hours nightly) produces cognitive impairment equivalent to legal intoxication after just two weeks – though subjective awareness of this decline remains minimal.

The consequences extend beyond daily functioning to long-term health. Studies reveal that chronic sleep insufficiency predicts increased risk of Alzheimer's disease, cardiovascular disease, metabolic disorders, and immune dysfunction – creating what sleep scientists call "accelerated aging syndrome." These physiological effects occur alongside what psychological researchers term "positive experience blunting" – diminished capacity to experience joy, interest, and connection due to emotional regulation impairment.

Three evidence-based strategies for restorative integration:

1. Implement Sleep Opportunity Protection: Research shows that deliberately allocating sufficient time for sleep (8-9 hours in bed) rather than focusing exclusively on sleep quality significantly improves both duration and restoration.
2. Practice Cognitive Downshifting Rituals: Studies demonstrate that establishing consistent pre-sleep routines that progressively reduce stimulation substantially enhances both sleep initiation and quality.
3. Develop Micro-Recovery Integration: Psychological research confirms that incorporating brief restorative periods throughout the day (10-20 minute relaxation intervals) creates cumulative benefits that complement nighttime sleep.

70. Not seeking help for mental health issues (depression, anxiety) when I needed it

This regret exemplifies what clinical psychologists call "psychological support avoidance" – resisting professional assistance despite experiencing significant mental health challenges. The psychological mechanism involves what stigma researchers term "internalized mental health prejudice" – applying more negative judgments to one's own psychological struggles than would be applied to others in similar circumstances.

This internalization creates what help-seeking researchers identify as "treatment ambivalence" – simultaneously suffering from symptoms while resisting interventions that could provide relief. Research demonstrates that this ambivalence stems from complex factors including vulnerability concerns, self-reliance values, outcome skepticism, and process misunderstandings – creating multifaceted barriers to assistance despite distress.

The consequences extend beyond sustained symptoms to life trajectory effects. Studies reveal that untreated mental health conditions create what developmental psychologists call "cascading constraint" – the progressive narrowing of educational, occupational, relational, and health outcomes as initial challenges affect multiple domains over time. This constraint occurs alongside what clinical researchers term "retroactive recognition" – the belated realization upon eventually receiving effective treatment that suffering was more preventable than previously understood.

Three evidence-based strategies for appropriate help-seeking:

1. Implement Symptom Objectification: Research shows that evaluating psychological challenges through external frameworks (validated screening tools, diagnostic criteria) significantly increases appropriate help-seeking by reducing subjective minimization.
2. Practice Treatment Benefit Education: Studies demonstrate that understanding specific success rates and mechanisms of psychological interventions substantially improves willingness to engage by replacing misconceptions with accurate expectations.
3. Develop Strength-Based Help Orientation: Psychological research confirms that reconceptualizing treatment-seeking as a sign of self-awareness and courage rather than weakness dramatically increases utilization among individuals with high self-reliance values.

71. Taking my good health for granted until it was gone

This regret reflects what health psychologists call "baseline health blindness" – insufficient appreciation for normal functioning until it becomes compromised. The psychological foundation involves what perceptual scientists term "adaptation-level phenomenon" – our tendency to establish current conditions as neutral reference points regardless of their objective value.

This adaptation creates what gratitude researchers identify as "health appreciation deficit" – the absence of conscious recognition for the remarkable capacities that enable daily activity. Research demonstrates that health typically operates as what attention theorists call a "background condition" – unnoticed unless disrupted, despite its fundamental enabling role for virtually all valued activities.

The consequences manifest primarily in missed experiential quality rather than objective health outcomes. Studies reveal that health appreciation correlates with what positive psychologists call "savoring capacity" – the ability to derive full enjoyment from positive experiences rather than taking them for granted. This capacity creates resilience against what meaning researchers term "post-capability regret" – the particularly painful awareness after health diminishment that available opportunities weren't fully utilized.

Three evidence-based strategies for health appreciation development:

1. Implement Functional Gratitude Practice: Research shows that regularly acknowledging specific bodily capacities (mobility, senses, absence of pain) significantly enhances both present enjoyment and motivates protective behaviors.

2. Practice Health-Enabled Activity Awareness: Studies demonstrate that periodically noting which valued activities depend on specific health aspects substantially increases appreciation without requiring health challenges as triggers.

3. Develop Physical Capacity Celebration: Psychological research confirms that deliberately creating opportunities to experience and enjoy bodily capabilities through movement, nature engagement, or sensory experiences builds durable appreciation that persists through minor limitations.

72. Not quitting bad habits (like smoking) sooner to protect my health

This regret exemplifies what behavioral economists call "temporal discounting reversal" – the retrospective recognition that future health was excessively devalued in previous decisions about harmful habits. The psychological mechanism involves what addiction researchers term "reward asymmetry" – immediate benefits of habits receiving disproportionate weight compared to delayed consequences despite their objectively greater significance.

This asymmetry creates what health behavior theorists identify as the "contemplation trap" – acknowledging a habit's harmfulness while repeatedly postponing change initiation. Research demonstrates that this postponement pattern stems from what psychologists call "present-self/future-self discontinuity" – perceiving our future selves as sufficiently separate entities that their welfare concerns us less than our present comfort.

The consequences extend beyond the specific health impacts to what regret researchers call "preventable contribution distress" – the particularly painful awareness that current suffering was partially self-initiated rather than entirely externally caused. Studies reveal that this awareness creates what meaning theorists term "agency regret" – a specific form of remorse centering on actions taken or not taken rather than circumstances beyond control.

Three evidence-based strategies for timely habit modification:

1. Implement Future-Self Connection: Research shows that creating concrete mental representations of your future self significantly reduces temporal discounting and increases protective behavior by enhancing perceived continuity.
2. Practice Regret Anticipation: Studies demonstrate that deliberately imagining future regret for current inaction substantially motivates present behavior change through what psychologists call "prospective retrospection."
3. Develop Success Pattern Recognition: Psychological research confirms that identifying previous successful behavior changes in any domain enhances self-efficacy for current challenges, creating confidence that counteracts discouraging predictions about capacity for change.

73. Overindulging and not practicing moderation (in food, drink, etc.)

This regret exemplifies what behavioral scientists call "hedonic regulation failure" – the systematic inability to balance pleasure-seeking with long-term well-being despite their interdependence. The psychological foundation involves what neuroscientists term "reward pathway hijacking" – modern substances and experiences providing supernormal stimulation that overwhelms evolved satiety mechanisms.

This stimulation creates what self-regulation researchers identify as "moderation threshold confusion" – difficulty distinguishing between enjoyment and excess when consumption patterns gradually intensify. Research demonstrates that healthy pleasure operates through what positive psychologists call "savoring mechanisms" – deriving maximum enjoyment from moderate experiences through mindful attention. Paradoxically, overconsumption often diminishes pleasure through neuroadaptation while simultaneously increasing health consequences.

The consequences extend beyond physical impacts to psychological functioning. Studies reveal that individuals with developed moderation skills report significantly higher life satisfaction than those exhibiting either deprivation or excess patterns. This satisfaction stems from what wellbeing researchers call "sustainable hedonism" – the capacity to enjoy pleasures in ways that enhance rather than compromise long-term flourishing.

Three evidence-based strategies for cultivating moderation:

1. Implement Enjoyment Enhancement Skills: Research shows that deliberately maximizing pleasure from smaller portions or experiences (eating slowly, eliminating distractions) creates greater satisfaction than mindless consumption, reducing quantity needs.

2. Practice Moderation Scheduling: Studies demonstrate that planned indulgences within clear boundaries significantly increase adherence to moderation by eliminating uncertainty and providing anticipated pleasure.

3. Develop Values-Based Decision Making: Psychological research confirms that evaluating consumption choices against explicitly identified life values substantially improves regulation by connecting immediate decisions to meaningful life goals.

74. Ignoring advice from doctors or loved ones about taking care of my health

This regret reflects what health psychologists call "recommendation resistance syndrome" – systematically disregarding credible health guidance despite its potential benefit. The psychological mechanism involves what cognitive scientists term "autonomy threat response" – interpreting advice as controlling rather than informative, triggering opposition regardless of content merit.

This interpretation creates what medical communication researchers identify as "reactance amplification" – increasing resistance proportionally to perceived pressure, even when that pressure comes from legitimate concern. Research demonstrates that health advice triggers what self-perception theorists call "identity-threat assessment" – evaluating guidance not merely for accuracy but for compatibility with how we view ourselves.

The consequences manifest in what preventive medicine specialists term "avoidable progression" – health conditions advancing from manageable to serious states through delayed intervention. Studies reveal that recommendation resistance often gives way to what accountability researchers call "retrospective responsibility acknowledgment" – the painful recognition when facing consequences that others' concerns were legitimate and dismissal was unwarranted.

Three evidence-based strategies for constructive advice engagement:

1. Implement Autonomy-Preserving Information Processing Research shows that deliberately focusing on health information content rather than delivery style

significantly enhances receptivity by separating useful guidance from perceived control attempts.

2. Practice Perspective-Taking Expansion: Studies demonstrate that considering health advice from the advisor's viewpoint—their legitimate care and concern—substantially improves openness by reframing recommendations as connection rather than control.

3. Develop Collaborative Assessment Approach: Psychological research confirms that actively participating in evaluating health information rather than passively receiving directions dramatically increases both acceptance and implementation through enhanced autonomy.

75. Sacrificing my health in pursuit of career success or other goals, only to suffer the consequences later

This regret exemplifies what organizational psychologists call "health-achievement trade-off syndrome" – systematically prioritizing external accomplishment over physical wellbeing despite their interdependence. The psychological foundation involves what value researchers term "delayed utility miscalculation" – drastically underestimating how central health becomes to life satisfaction as we age.

This miscalculation creates what work-life researchers identify as "sustainability illusion" – the false belief that current work patterns can continue indefinitely without biological consequences. Research demonstrates that achievement-oriented individuals often exhibit what performance psychologists call "physical invulnerability bias" – the tendency to view bodily limitations as applying to others but not themselves until evidence becomes undeniable.

The consequences extend beyond specific health conditions to identity disruption. Studies reveal that health crises following achievement-prioritization often trigger what meaning researchers term "value recalibration" – a profound shift in what matters that highlights the hollow nature of accomplishments that compromised wellbeing. This recalibration frequently produces what philosophical psychologists call "tragic irony recognition" – the painful awareness that health sacrificed for achievement ultimately prevented enjoying that achievement's rewards.

Three evidence-based strategies for sustainable achievement:

1. Implement Success-Health Integration Planning: Research shows that deliberately designing achievement paths that enhance rather than compromise physical wellbeing creates superior long-term outcomes in both domains.

2. Practice Sustainable Pace Setting: Studies demonstrate that establishing work rhythms that incorporate adequate recovery significantly improves both performance quality and longevity compared to continuous high-intensity effort.

3. Develop Achievement-Health Complementarity: Psychological research confirms that identifying ways career success can enhance health (resources for preventive care, schedule flexibility, meaning-based stress resilience) substantially improves balance by highlighting synergy rather than competition between domains.

76. Not living in the present moment (always dwelling on the past or worrying about the future)

This regret exemplifies what cognitive psychologists call "temporal displacement syndrome" – the habitual orientation of consciousness away from present experience toward either past memories or future projections. The psychological mechanism involves what neuroscientists term "default mode network dominance" – the brain's tendency to engage in self-referential thought rather than direct experiential awareness when not deliberately focused.

This dominance creates what mindfulness researchers identify as "experiential avoidance" – the systematic withdrawal from direct engagement with current reality despite its unique accessibility. Research demonstrates that present-moment awareness activates neural networks associated with sensory processing and positive affect while deactivating regions implicated in rumination and anxiety – producing what psychologists call "direct experience" of life rather than conceptual or narrative processing.

The consequences extend beyond missed enjoyment to psychological functioning. Studies reveal that individuals with greater present-moment capacity demonstrate enhanced relationship satisfaction, stress resilience, and overall well-being compared to those predominantly oriented toward past or future. This well-being derives from what consciousness researchers call "experiential richness" – the fuller, more textured quality of life available only through present engagement.

Three evidence-based strategies for present-moment engagement:

1. Implement Attention Anchoring Practices: Research confirms that deliberately focusing on immediate sensory experience (breath, sounds, physical sensations) for brief periods throughout the day substantially strengthens present-moment awareness capacity.
2. Practice "Cognitive Defusion Techniques": Studies demonstrate that learning to observe thoughts rather than becoming absorbed in them significantly enhances ability to remain present despite mental activity.
3. Develop "Transition Mindfulness": Psychological research shows that creating brief awareness pauses between activities dramatically improves present-moment engagement by interrupting automatic thought patterns that perpetuate temporal displacement.

77. Not cultivating mindfulness or practices to find calm and clarity

This regret reflects what contemplative researchers call "mental regulation deficit" – insufficient development of attentional control and emotional equilibrium despite their centrality to psychological well-being. The psychological foundation involves what neuroscientists term "untrained default response" – allowing mental patterns to operate automatically rather than cultivating deliberate relationship with consciousness.

This default creates what mindfulness scientists identify as "stimulus-reaction automaticity" – the habitual sequence of perception immediately triggering thought and emotion without the spaciousness of awareness. Research demonstrates that contemplative practices develop what neuropsychologists call "response flexibility" – the capacity to insert conscious choice between stimulus and reaction, creating psychological freedom unavailable to those without such training.

The consequences manifest in what emotional researchers term "affective volatility" – greater reactivity to circumstances with diminished recovery capacity. Studies reveal that individuals with established contemplative practices demonstrate enhanced emotional regulation, sustained attention, and cognitive flexibility compared to non-practitioners – creating what psychologists call "adaptive responding" rather than automatic reactivity.

Three evidence-based strategies for mental cultivation:

1. Implement Micromeditation Practice: Research shows that brief mindfulness periods (2-5 minutes) practiced consistently throughout daily life significantly develop contemplative capacity while minimizing time barriers.
2. Practice Mental Noting Technique: Studies demonstrate that simply labeling experiences ("thinking," "planning," "worrying") creates metacognitive awareness that interrupts identification with mental content.
3. Develop Environmental Mindfulness Cues: Psychological research confirms that establishing specific triggers for present-moment awareness (like doorways, phone rings, or red lights) significantly increases daily mindfulness by leveraging existing environmental patterns.

78. Neglecting my spiritual side and deeper questions of meaning

This regret exemplifies what existential psychologists call "meaning deficit disorder" – insufficient engagement with life's fundamental questions despite their importance for psychological integration. The psychological mechanism involves what cognitive scientists term "pragmatic dominance" – allowing immediate practical concerns to consistently override contemplation of broader meaning frameworks.

This dominance creates what developmental researchers identify as "existential foreclosure" – prematurely settling life's meaning questions without adequate exploration, often through default adoption of cultural narratives. Research demonstrates that meaning exploration activates what positive psychologists call "transcendent meaning-making" – connecting personal experience to broader frameworks that provide coherence, purpose, and significance beyond immediate circumstances.

The consequences extend beyond philosophical uncertainty to psychological functioning. Studies reveal that individuals with developed meaning systems demonstrate greater resilience during adversity, enhanced prosocial behavior, and superior mortality outcomes compared to those with meaning deficits. This advantage stems from what meaning researchers call "existential resources" – psychological assets that provide stability during uncertainty and suffering.

Three evidence-based strategies for meaning development:

1. Implement Sacred Time Protection: Research shows that deliberately allocating regular periods for contemplative exploration significantly enhances meaning development by creating space for deeper consideration unavailable in busy daily life.
2. Practice Ultimate Concern Inquiry: Studies demonstrate that periodically examining core questions (What matters most? What gives my life meaning? What continues after I'm gone?) develops existential intelligence even without definitive answers.
3. Develop Meaning Community Engagement: Psychological research confirms that participating in groups focused on life's deeper questions substantially enhances meaning formation through dialogue, diverse perspectives, and shared exploration.

79. Not exploring or connecting with my faith/spiritual beliefs more fully

This regret reflects what religious psychologists call "spiritual potential gap" – the distance between one's spiritual inclinations and their actual development or expression. The psychological foundation involves what motivation researchers term "spiritual procrastination" – postponing deeper engagement with transcendent dimensions despite their felt importance.

This procrastination creates what contemplative scientists identify as "belief-practice incongruence" – holding spiritual values or beliefs without the transformative practices that actualize them. Research demonstrates that spiritual engagement requires what religious development specialists call "spiritual disciplines" – regular practices that deepen connection to transcendent dimensions beyond intellectual assent to beliefs.

The consequences manifest in what meaning researchers term "spiritual thinness" – possessing spiritual frameworks without sufficient depth to provide genuine existential resources. Studies reveal that individuals who actively engage spiritual practices within their tradition demonstrate enhanced psychological well-being, community connection, and existential security compared to those with merely nominal affiliation.

Three evidence-based strategies for spiritual deepening:

1. Implement Practice-Based Spirituality: Research shows that emphasizing experiential spiritual practices (meditation, prayer, contemplation) rather than solely intellectual beliefs significantly enhances meaningful spiritual connection.
2. Practice Sacred Reading Approach: Studies demonstrate that engaging spiritual texts contemplatively rather than merely informatively—reading smaller portions with reflection—substantially deepens spiritual integration.
3. Develop Spiritual Community Embeddedness: Psychological research confirms that active participation in communities sharing spiritual values dramatically enhances individual spiritual development through support, accountability, and shared wisdom.

80. Not making peace with my past and carrying old wounds for too long

This regret exemplifies what trauma psychologists call "psychological encapsulation" – the persistent isolation of painful experiences from integration with broader life narrative. The psychological mechanism involves what cognitive scientists term "memory reconsolidation failure" – the inability to update emotional learning from past events with new information and perspective.

This failure creates what clinical researchers identify as "narrative fragmentation" – the inability to construct coherent life stories that incorporate difficult experiences within meaningful frameworks. Research demonstrates that psychological healing requires what narrative therapists call "meaning reconstruction" – reinterpreting painful events within broader contexts that acknowledge both suffering and resilience.

The consequences extend beyond emotional discomfort to identity formation. Studies reveal that individuals who successfully integrate difficult experiences demonstrate enhanced psychological complexity, greater meaning-making capability, and superior resilience compared to those with unprocessed trauma. This integration produces what post-traumatic growth researchers call "adversity-based wisdom" – deeper understanding derived from working through rather than avoiding painful experiences.

Three evidence-based strategies for historical integration:

1. Implement Compassionate Witnessing Practice: Research shows that deliberately revisiting difficult experiences with self-compassion significantly facilitates integration by providing the emotional safety necessary for processing.
2. Practice "Narrative Reconstruction": Studies demonstrate that deliberately creating coherent stories of difficult experiences with beginning, middle, and meaningful resolution substantially enhances psychological healing.
3. Develop "Wisdom Extraction": Psychological research confirms that explicitly identifying lessons, strengths, and values that emerged from suffering creates redemptive narratives that transform painful histories into psychological resources.

81. Holding onto anger and resentment instead of forgiving

This regret reflects what forgiveness researchers call "emotional hostage syndrome" – remaining psychologically bound to offenders through sustained negative emotion despite its self-harming effects. The psychological foundation involves what justice theorists term "punishment illusion" – the mistaken belief that maintaining resentment somehow affects offenders when it primarily impacts the holder.

This illusion creates what clinical psychologists identify as "rumination trap" — repetitive thought patterns that perpetuate anger and prevent emotional resolution. Research demonstrates that forgiveness operates through what psychologists call "emotional uncoupling" — releasing the psychological bonds that tie one's well-being to offenders' acknowledgment or suffering.

The consequences extend beyond emotional distress to physical health. Meta-analyses reveal significant associations between forgiveness and cardiovascular health, immune function, and pain perception — creating what health psychologists call "embodied resentment" with measurable physiological costs. These findings align with what Buddhist psychology terms "second arrow suffering" — the additional self-inflicted pain beyond the original injury.

Three evidence-based strategies for forgiveness development:

1. Implement Forgiveness Reframing: Research confirms that understanding forgiveness as emotional release for personal benefit rather than moral pardon for offenders significantly increases willingness to engage forgiveness processes.
2. Practice Perspective-Taking Expansion: Studies demonstrate that deliberately considering contextual factors influencing harmful behavior substantially facilitates forgiveness by reducing attributions of pure malice.
3. Develop Incremental Forgiveness Process: Psychological research shows that approaching forgiveness as a gradual process rather than a single decision dramatically enhances success by accommodating the complex emotional processing forgiveness requires.

82. Not forgiving myself for my own mistakes and shortcomings

This regret exemplifies what self-compassion researchers call "internal relationship disorder" — maintaining a persistently harsh, punitive stance toward oneself despite its detrimental effects on psychological functioning. The psychological mechanism involves what attributional theorists term "characterological self-blame" — interpreting mistakes as evidence of fundamental defectiveness rather than specific behaviors in context.

This interpretation creates what clinical psychologists identify as "shame-based identity" — organizing self-concept around perceived inadequacy rather than inherent worthiness with imperfections. Research demonstrates that self-forgiveness operates through what positive psychologists call "compassionate responsibility" – acknowledging mistakes while maintaining fundamental self-worth and commitment to growth.

The consequences manifest in what motivation researchers term "avoidance-based regulation" – organizing behavior around preventing failure rather than pursuing meaningful goals. Studies reveal that individuals with greater self-compassion demonstrate enhanced psychological resilience, reduced depression/anxiety, and greater willingness to acknowledge mistakes compared to self-critical individuals.

Three evidence-based strategies for self-forgiveness cultivation:

1. Implement Common Humanity Practice: Research shows that deliberately recognizing the universality of human imperfection significantly reduces shame by contextualizing personal failings within shared human experience.
2. Practice Self-Compassionate Responsibility: Studies demonstrate that combining genuine accountability for mistakes with kind understanding of human limitation substantially enhances genuine self-forgiveness.
3. Develop Growth-Commitment Pathways: Psychological research confirms that creating concrete plans to learn from mistakes dramatically reduces self-punishment by redirecting energy from criticism to constructive change.

83. Being too caught up in material things and neglecting my values and soul

This regret reflects what value psychologists call "extrinsic dominance syndrome" – organizing life primarily around external rewards (wealth, possessions, status) rather than intrinsic satisfactions (meaning, growth, connection). The psychological foundation involves what motivation researchers term "hedonic treadmill entrapment" – pursuing acquisitions that provide diminishing returns while requiring increasing investment.

This entrapment creates what spiritual psychologists identify as "soul neglect" – insufficient attention to deeper dimensions of existence that provide genuine fulfillment. Research demonstrates that materialism correlates negatively with multiple well-being indicators, creating what consumer psychologists call "affluenza" – psychological impoverishment amid material abundance.

The consequences extend beyond psychological dissatisfaction to relational impacts. Studies reveal that higher materialism predicts lower-quality relationships, reduced empathy, and diminished community involvement – creating what social scientists term "transactional orientation" toward human connections. This orientation undermines what meaning researchers identify as "eudemonic well-being" – fulfillment derived from living in accordance with deeper values and purpose.

Three evidence-based strategies for values-based living:

1. Implement Values Clarification Exercise: Research confirms that explicitly identifying core personal values significantly enhances decision alignment with deeper priorities rather than cultural defaults.
2. Practice Gratitude Amplification: Studies demonstrate that regular appreciation of existing resources substantially reduces hedonic adaptation and acquisition-seeking by highlighting current sufficiency.
3. Develop Experiential Investment Shift: Psychological research shows that deliberately directing resources toward meaningful experiences rather than possessions significantly enhances subjective well-being and life satisfaction.

84. Compromising my integrity or ethics for short-term gains and regretting it later

This regret exemplifies what moral psychologists call "ethical fading syndrome" – the progressive diminishment of ethical dimensions in decision-making despite their importance for psychological coherence. The psychological mechanism involves what behavioral economists term "hyperbolic discounting" – systematically overvaluing immediate benefits while undervaluing delayed consequences, including self-concept impacts.

This discounting creates what integrity researchers identify as "moral self-discrepancy" – incongruence between actual behavior and ethical self-image that generates what psychologists call "moral emotions" like guilt and shame. Research demonstrates that integrity functions as what identity theorists call "self-coherence maintenance" – preserving alignment between values and actions essential for psychological well-being.

The consequences extend beyond immediate emotional discomfort to narrative identity. Studies reveal that ethical compromises create what meaning researchers call "biographical discontinuity" – disruptions in life story coherence that undermine sense of self-consistency across time. This discontinuity threatens what developmental psychologists identify as "ego integrity" – the late-life task of viewing one's life as worthwhile and reasonably consistent with core values.

Three evidence-based strategies for integrity maintenance:

1. Implement Pre-commitment Strategy: Research shows that establishing ethical boundaries before encountering specific temptations significantly enhances decision quality by removing in-the-moment rationalization.
2. Practice Moral Identity Activation: Studies demonstrate that deliberately accessing ethical values before decisions substantially improves moral choice by making ethical dimensions more salient than immediate benefits.
3. Develop Integrity Partnership: Psychological research confirms that cultivating relationships with individuals who share core values dramatically enhances ethical consistency through accountability and support during challenging situations.

85. Not aligning my life with my core values and what truly mattered to me

This regret reflects what existential psychologists call "authenticity deficit" – the persistent misalignment between deeper values and actual life patterns despite its impact on psychological fulfillment. The psychological foundation involves what decision researchers term "choice point blindness" – failing to recognize pivotal moments where values could direct decisions rather than default patterns.

This blindness creates what developmental psychologists identify as "false-self living" – organizing behavior around external expectations rather than internal values. Research demonstrates that alignment between values and actions produces what positive psychologists call "authenticity" – the subjective experience of self-congruence associated with enhanced well-being across multiple domains.

The consequences manifest in what meaning researchers term "existential vacuum" – the sense of emptiness that develops when life lacks compelling purpose despite external achievements. Studies reveal that individuals with greater value-behavior alignment report significantly higher life satisfaction, meaning, and lower regret intensity compared to those exhibiting value-behavior gaps.

Three evidence-based strategies for values alignment:

1. Implement Values-Action Audit: Research confirms that periodically reviewing how time, energy, and resources align with stated values significantly enhances congruence by identifying specific misalignment patterns.
2. Practice Micro-Alignment Decisions: Studies demonstrate that focusing on small daily choices rather than major life changes substantially improves values-congruence through accumulated impact of consistent small actions.
3. Develop Legacy Perspective: Psychological research shows that periodically considering how you wish to be remembered dramatically clarifies values and motivates alignment by highlighting long-term rather than immediate consequences of choices.

86. Letting fear and constant worry rob me of the joy I could have had

This regret exemplifies what anxiety researchers call "anticipatory suffering syndrome" – experiencing negative emotions about potential future events regardless of their actual occurrence. The psychological mechanism involves what cognitive scientists term "negative simulation bias" – the tendency to mentally rehearse worst-case scenarios while underestimating coping capacity.

This bias creates what mindfulness researchers identify as "present-moment extraction" – the habitual withdrawal from current experience into mental projections about threatening futures. Research demonstrates that chronic worry activates neural stress responses identical to actual threats, producing what health psychologists call "anticipatory stress response" with measurable physiological costs despite the absence of actual danger.

The consequences extend beyond subjective distress to experiential capacity. Studies reveal that worry significantly impairs ability to experience positive emotion through what emotion researchers call "positive-negative attentional asymmetry" – greater cognitive resources allocated to threat monitoring than opportunity awareness. This asymmetry creates what positive psychologists term "preemptive joy suppression" – diminished capacity to experience pleasure due to hypervigilance about potential negative outcomes.

Three evidence-based strategies for worry reduction:

1. Implement Productive Worry Period: Research shows that containing worry to specific time periods significantly reduces its interference with present enjoyment by providing structured outlet while limiting mental intrusion.

2. Practice Worry Outcome Analysis: Studies demonstrate that systematically tracking worry predictions against actual outcomes substantially reduces worry by highlighting its poor predictive accuracy and unnecessary emotional cost.

3. Develop Threat-Joy Balance: Psychological research confirms that deliberately cultivating positive experiences alongside legitimate concern creates emotional resilience unavailable through either worry reduction or positive focus alone.

87. Not taking the time for gratitude and appreciating the blessings I had

This regret exemplifies what positive psychologists call "appreciation deficit disorder" – the systematic failure to notice and savor positive aspects of experience despite their abundance. The psychological mechanism involves what attention researchers term "negativity bias" – our evolutionary tendency to allocate disproportionate cognitive resources to potential threats rather than benefits, creating perceptual distortion.

This bias creates what wellbeing scientists identify as "hedonic perception asymmetry" – noticing absences and problems more readily than presences and pleasures. Research demonstrates that gratitude functions as what we call a "cognitive reorientation strategy" – deliberately redirecting attention toward positive aspects of experience that would otherwise go unnoticed due to adaptation.

The consequences of this attention misdirection extend beyond momentary happiness to broader life satisfaction. Studies reveal that individuals who practice regular gratitude demonstrate significantly higher levels of subjective wellbeing, enhanced relationship quality, and superior physical health outcomes compared to those who don't. This impact stems from what we call "appreciative encoding" – the neural process of registering positive experiences deeply enough to counter negativity dominance.

Three evidence-based strategies for gratitude cultivation:

1. Implement Three Blessings Practice: Research shows that documenting three positive events daily with their causes significantly increases happiness and decreases depression for up to six months.
2. Practice Gratitude Reframing: Studies demonstrate that deliberately identifying benefits within challenges substantially enhances resilience by activating appreciative pathways alongside problem-solving processes.
3. Develop Counterfactual Gratitude: Psychological research confirms that periodically considering how circumstances could be worse generates profound appreciation for current reality, effectively counteracting adaptation to positives.

88. Failing to see or appreciate the beauty in life (nature, art, everyday moments)

This regret reflects what consciousness researchers call "aesthetic attention blindness" – diminished awareness of beauty and wonder despite their psychological importance. The psychological foundation involves what cognitive scientists term "utilitarian perception" – processing environments primarily for practical information rather than aesthetic or meaningful dimensions.

This processing creates what contemplative researchers identify as "beauty bypassing" – moving through aesthetically rich environments without engaging their emotional and spiritual potential. Research demonstrates that beauty appreciation activates what neuroscientists call the "awe response" – a distinct neural state associated with expanded perception, diminished self-preoccupation, and enhanced connectedness.

The consequences extend beyond missed pleasure to cognitive functioning. Studies in environmental psychology reveal that experiences of natural beauty provide what attention researchers call "cognitive restoration" – replenishing directed attention capacity depleted by focused tasks. This restoration represents one dimension of what positive psychologists term "transcendent emotions" – experiences like awe and elevation that connect individuals to something larger than themselves.

Three evidence-based strategies for beauty engagement:

1. Implement Aesthetic Attention Training: Research confirms that deliberate practice noticing visual, auditory, and sensory beauty significantly enhances perception capacity and associated positive emotions.

2. Practice Awe Walks: Studies demonstrate that walking with intentional openness to wonder and beauty substantially increases wellbeing, humility, and prosocial orientation compared to utilitarian walking.

3. Develop Savoring Through Sharing: Psychological research shows that communicating beautiful experiences to others, whether immediately or later, significantly enhances their emotional impact through elaborative encoding.

89. Not showing more kindness and empathy to others when I had the chance

This regret exemplifies what compassion researchers call "prosocial opportunity neglect" – failing to act on possibilities for kindness despite their dual benefit for recipients and givers. The psychological mechanism involves what social psychologists term "diffusion of responsibility" – diminished sense of personal obligation to help in the absence of explicit expectations.

This diffusion creates what moral psychologists identify as "ethical fading" – the gradual disappearance of compassionate action as an option from conscious awareness. Research demonstrates that kindness generates what neuroscientists call "helper's high" – activation of reward pathways through helping others that creates genuine positive emotion for the giver while benefiting recipients.

The consequences extend beyond individual interactions to personality development. Studies reveal that regular compassionate action produces what character researchers call "virtue consolidation" – the gradual integration of prosocial behavior into identity through consistent practice. This consolidation enhances what self-perception theorists term "moral self-concept" – a core aspect of identity associated with meaning, purpose, and self-respect.

Three evidence-based strategies for compassion cultivation:

1. Implement Daily Kindness Intention: Research shows that beginning each day by identifying specific opportunities for compassion significantly increases prosocial behavior through heightened awareness of helping possibilities.

2. Practice Empathic Perspective-Taking: Studies demonstrate that deliberately imagining others' experiences substantially enhances helping motivation by reducing psychological distance and activating care responses.

3. Develop Kindness Habit Formation: Psychological research confirms that linking compassionate acts to existing routines dramatically increases consistency by leveraging established behavioral patterns as implementation triggers.

90. Not addressing deep emotional hurts or traumas, leaving them unresolved

This regret reflects what trauma researchers call "emotional encapsulation syndrome" – the isolation of painful experiences from integration with broader life narrative. The psychological foundation involves what neuroscientists term "avoidance reinforcement" – the immediate relief of sidestepping difficult emotions inadvertently strengthening future avoidance despite long-term costs.

This reinforcement creates what clinical psychologists identify as "affect phobia" – fear of certain emotional states that prevents their processing and resolution. Research demonstrates that emotional healing requires what we call "facilitated exposure" – approaching difficult feelings within supportive contexts that enable processing without overwhelming adaptive capacity.

The consequences manifest in what developmental scientists call "emotional compartmentalization" – the fragmentation of experience that diminishes psychological coherence and flexibility. Studies reveal that unresolved trauma creates neuroendocrine dysregulation and cognitive patterns associated with various physical and psychological conditions – what medical researchers term "embodied distress" in recognition of mind-body interconnection.

Three evidence-based strategies for emotional resolution:

1. Implement Graduated Emotional Approach: Research confirms that addressing difficult feelings in progressive steps substantially increases processing success by respecting individual tolerance thresholds.

2. Practice Compassionate Witness Stance: Studies demonstrate that engaging painful experiences with self-kindness rather than self-judgment significantly enhances integration capacity through reduced defensive responses.

3. Develop Therapeutic Support Utilization: Psychological research shows that appropriate professional guidance dramatically improves trauma resolution outcomes by providing both expertise and interpersonal safety necessary for deep processing.

91. Never finding a sense of inner calm or acceptance until the very end

This regret exemplifies what contemplative researchers call "equanimity deficit" – insufficient development of internal stability despite its centrality to psychological flourishing. The psychological mechanism involves what attention scientists term "resistance preoccupation" – investing mental resources in fighting reality rather than responding constructively within its parameters.

This preoccupation creates what mindfulness researchers identify as "reactivity loop" – the escalation of distress through secondary responses to primary difficulties. Research demonstrates that acceptance operates through what neuroscientists call "adaptive disengagement" – releasing unhelpful struggle without resignation, creating psychological freedom unavailable through either resistance or surrender.

The consequences extend beyond subjective distress to decision quality. Studies reveal that emotional equanimity enhances what cognitive scientists call "response flexibility" – the capacity to select optimal actions rather than reactions driven by emotional reactivity. This flexibility produces what psychological researchers term "constructed peace" – tranquility that results from skilled mental response rather than favorable circumstances.

Three evidence-based strategies for cultivating equanimity:

1. Implement Acceptance Practice: Research shows that deliberately acknowledging reality as it exists before problem-solving significantly reduces emotional reactivity while enhancing constructive response capacity.
2. Practice Equanimity Meditation: Studies demonstrate that regularly cultivating mental balance during minor irritations substantially improves capacity to maintain equilibrium during major challenges.
3. Develop Wisdom Perspective: Psychological research confirms that considering situations from expanded temporal and significance frames dramatically enhances calm by revealing which matters deserve emotional investment and which don't.

92. Not learning to love and accept myself, spending too much of life in self-doubt or shame

This regret reflects what self-compassion researchers call "internal relationship disorder" – the persistent pattern of harsh self-judgment that creates psychological suffering and developmental constraint. The psychological foundation involves what attribution theorists term "self-directed fundamental attribution error" – applying stricter standards and more negative interpretations to oneself than to others in similar circumstances.

This asymmetry creates what clinical psychologists identify as "core shame" – the belief in fundamental inadequacy rather than specific improvable behaviors. Research demonstrates that self-compassion activates what neuroscientists call "caregiving neural circuitry" – brain regions associated with nurturing that can be directed toward oneself, generating security and resilience unavailable through achievement or external validation alone.

The consequences manifest in what motivational researchers term "defensive self-regulation" – organizing behavior around avoiding failure rather than approaching meaningful goals. Studies reveal that individuals with greater self-compassion demonstrate enhanced psychological resilience, greater willingness to acknowledge mistakes, and superior emotional recovery compared to those with self-critical patterns.

Three evidence-based strategies for self-compassion development:

1. Implement Self-Kindness Practice: Research confirms that deliberately speaking to yourself as you would to a valued friend when facing difficulties significantly reduces shame while enhancing constructive behavior.
2. Practice Common Humanity Recognition: Studies demonstrate that acknowledging the universal nature of struggle and imperfection substantially reduces isolation and inadequacy beliefs that intensify suffering.
3. Develop Growth-Oriented Self-Coaching: Psychological research shows that combining genuine acceptance of current reality with specific improvement pathways creates motivational effectiveness superior to either criticism or complacency alone.

Chapter 8. Contributions & Legacy

93. Not making a positive difference in the lives of others

This regret exemplifies what meaning researchers call "contribution deficit" – insufficient investment in prosocial impact despite its centrality to psychological well-being. The psychological mechanism involves what developmental scientists term "generativity failure" – not fulfilling the fundamental human need to contribute to others' welfare and growth that emerges prominently in midlife.

This failure creates what purpose researchers identify as "significance vacuum" – the absence of evidence that one's existence positively affected others' lives. Research demonstrates that contribution functions as what positive psychologists call a "meaning amplifier" – substantially enhancing life satisfaction beyond what personal accomplishment alone provides through what we term "self-transcendent purpose."

The consequences extend beyond subjective fulfillment to physical health. Studies reveal that individuals with stronger contribution orientation demonstrate enhanced immune function, reduced inflammatory markers, and greater longevity compared to those primarily focused on self-interest. This advantage stems from what health psychologists call "purpose-driven physiology" – the biological benefits of living beyond self-focused concerns.

Three evidence-based strategies for contribution integration:

1. Implement Signature Strength Redirection: Research shows that identifying your core strengths and deliberately applying them toward helping others significantly enhances both impact and personal fulfillment compared to generic helping.
2. Practice Micro-Contribution Habit Formation: Studies demonstrate that establishing small, regular helping behaviors substantially increases prosocial engagement by creating foundation patterns that can expand over time.
3. Develop Contribution Vision Planning: Psychological research confirms that explicitly identifying how you hope your life improves others' welfare dramatically increases motivation and follow-through on prosocial intentions.

94. Not leaving behind a legacy or impact I could be proud of

This regret reflects what existential psychologists call "symbolic immortality deficit" – insufficient creation of enduring impact that extends one's influence beyond biological life. The psychological foundation involves what mortality researchers term "finitude anxiety" – the natural human concern about life's temporal limitations that drives creation of lasting contributions.

This anxiety creates what developmental scientists identify as "generative urgency" – the increasing motivation to establish meaningful legacy as mortality awareness heightens. Research demonstrates that legacy consideration activates what values theorists call "transcendent time perspective" – extending decision-making beyond immediate outcomes to include impacts that outlast one's lifetime.

The consequences manifest in what meaning researchers term "existential evaluation" – the assessment of one's life as significant beyond its temporal boundaries. Studies reveal that individuals with identifiable legacies report significantly higher life satisfaction and reduced death anxiety compared to those without clear ongoing impact – creating what psychologists call "symbolic continuity" that addresses fundamental concerns about life's finitude.

Three evidence-based strategies for legacy development:

1. Implement Legacy Audit: Research shows that periodically examining your life for elements that will continue beyond you significantly enhances intentional creation of meaningful ongoing impact.
2. Practice Values Transmission: Studies demonstrate that deliberately identifying and communicating core values to younger generations creates enduring influence that substantially outlasts material contributions.
3. Develop Contribution Documentation: Psychological research confirms that recording wisdom, stories, or lessons learned creates accessible resources that extend influence beyond direct interaction, effectively expanding impact across time.

95. Not giving back to my community or volunteering my time

This regret exemplifies what social psychologists call "community connection deficit" – insufficient engagement with collective welfare despite its benefits for both community and individual. The psychological mechanism involves what sociologists term "civic disengagement" – the progressive withdrawal from community participation that characterizes modern individualistic societies.

This disengagement creates what belonging researchers identify as "community attachment erosion" – the weakening of meaningful connection to place and people that provides essential psychological grounding. Research demonstrates that community service functions as what positive psychologists call a "wellbeing multiplier" – simultaneously addressing fundamental needs for belonging, purpose, competence, and positive relationship.

The consequences extend beyond personal benefits to collective functioning. Studies reveal that communities with higher volunteerism demonstrate greater resilience during challenges, enhanced social capital, and improved collective efficacy compared to those with participation deficits. This advantage stems from what systems theorists call "reciprocal resource mobilization" – the enhanced capacity to address needs that emerges through cooperative engagement.

Three evidence-based strategies for community engagement:

1. Implement Interest-Based Volunteering: Research confirms that selecting service opportunities aligned with personal interests dramatically increases sustained involvement compared to obligation-driven participation.
2. Practice Time-Bounded Commitment: Studies demonstrate that starting with clearly defined, limited-duration volunteer roles substantially reduces barriers to initial engagement while providing experience that often motivates continued involvement.
3. Develop Contribution Partnerships: Psychological research shows that volunteering with friends or family significantly enhances both consistency and satisfaction by combining social connection with service impact.

96. Not donating or contributing to causes I truly cared about

This regret reflects what prosocial researchers call "values-action gap" – the discrepancy between causes identified as personally important and actual resource allocation. The psychological foundation involves what behavioral economists term "psychological distance effect" – the diminished emotional impact of abstract needs compared to immediate, visible concerns despite their objective importance.

This distance creates what philanthropy researchers identify as "compassion fade" – reduced motivation to help as issues become more statistical rather than individual and personal. Research demonstrates that financial contribution activates what neuroscientists call the "helper's high" – reward circuitry activation similar to that experienced during direct helping behavior that enhances subjective wellbeing.

The consequences manifest in what values psychologists term "integrity deficit" – the uncomfortable awareness of discrepancy between stated values and actual behavior. Studies reveal that individuals who align financial resources with deeply held values report significantly greater life satisfaction and reduced internal conflict compared to those exhibiting values-spending misalignment.

Three evidence-based strategies for aligned contribution:

1. **Implement Value-Based Budgeting**: Research shows that proactively allocating specific financial resources to meaningful causes substantially increases follow-through on philanthropic intentions.
2. **Practice Psychological Distance Reduction**: Studies demonstrate that connecting with specific individuals affected by causes dramatically enhances giving motivation by converting statistical concerns to emotionally resonant human impact.
3. **Develop Giving Rituals**: Psychological research confirms that establishing consistent giving patterns tied to specific events (birthdays, holidays, anniversaries) significantly increases contribution consistency through habit formation.

97. Not being a mentor or guiding the next generation when I could have

This regret exemplifies what developmental psychologists call "generative mentorship gap" – insufficient transmission of accumulated wisdom and support despite its value for both recipient and provider. The psychological mechanism involves what social scientists term "expertise blindness" – underestimating the value of one's knowledge and experience that leads to withholding guidance that could benefit others.

This blindness creates what identity researchers identify as "wisdom transmission failure" – the interrupted flow of hard-earned insights that could otherwise benefit subsequent generations. Research demonstrates that mentoring activates what positive psychologists call "generativity fulfillment" – satisfaction of the fundamental developmental need to guide others that emerges prominently in middle and later adulthood.

The consequences extend beyond lost knowledge transmission to identity formation. Studies reveal that individuals who engage in mentoring relationships demonstrate enhanced meaning, purpose, and legacy perception compared to those with comparable expertise who don't mentor – creating what developmental theorists term "generative accomplishment" that contributes significantly to psychological flourishing.

Three evidence-based strategies for mentorship engagement:

1. Implement Knowledge Inventory Assessment: Research confirms that systematically identifying your unique expertise significantly enhances recognition of mentoring opportunities that might otherwise be overlooked.
2. Practice Graduated Guidance Approach: Studies demonstrate that beginning with limited-scope mentoring substantially reduces initiation barriers while providing experience that builds confidence for deeper engagement.
3. Develop Structured Mentorship Agreements: Psychological research shows that establishing clear expectations and boundaries dramatically improves mentoring relationship quality and sustainability for both parties.

98. Not sharing my knowledge, story, or wisdom to help or inspire others

This regret reflects what narrative psychologists call "wisdom sequestration" – keeping accumulated insights private despite their potential value to others. The psychological foundation involves what social researchers term "impact underestimation" – systematically misjudging how much one's experiences and perspectives could benefit others.

This underestimation creates what communication theorists identify as "wisdom bottleneck" – the restriction of potentially valuable insights to a single individual rather than allowing their broader application. Research demonstrates that wisdom sharing activates what meaning researchers call "life coherence enhancement" – the increased sense of significance and pattern that emerges when reflecting on life lessons for others' benefit.

The consequences manifest in what generativity theorists term "unused resource atrophy" – the gradual fading of accumulated insights that occurs without the reinforcement and refinement that sharing provides. Studies reveal that individuals who actively share their wisdom report significantly greater purpose fulfillment and identity integration compared to those who retain similar insights without transmission.

Three evidence-based strategies for wisdom sharing:

1. Implement Experience-to-Insight Reflection: Research shows that deliberately extracting learnings from significant life experiences significantly enhances capacity to share meaningful wisdom rather than merely recounting events.
2. Practice Contextual Wisdom Communication: Studies demonstrate that sharing insights in response to others' expressed needs substantially increases both receptivity and perceived value compared to unsolicited advice.
3. Develop Wisdom Documentation Habits: Psychological research confirms that recording insights in accessible formats (writing, recording, digital sharing) dramatically extends potential impact beyond immediate social circles and temporal limitations.

99. Not creating anything that would outlast me (like art, writing, or projects)

This regret exemplifies what creative psychologists call "generative expression deficit" – insufficient manifestation of internal capabilities into enduring external forms. The psychological mechanism involves what motivational scientists term "creation postponement" – the perpetual delay of creative action despite persistent desire to produce lasting works.

This postponement creates what developmental researchers identify as "creative legacy vacancy" – the absence of tangible creations that embody one's unique perspective and capabilities beyond biological life. Research demonstrates that creative production fulfills what existential psychologists call "symbolic immortality needs" – the desire to transcend physical mortality through works that continue to affect others beyond one's lifetime.

The consequences extend beyond legacy perception to present wellbeing. Studies reveal that individuals engaged in creating potentially enduring works report significantly higher levels of flow experience, purpose, and life satisfaction compared to those with similar creative impulses left unexpressed – producing what creativity researchers term "manifestation fulfillment" unavailable through mere ideation.

Three evidence-based strategies for creative manifestation:

1. Implement Micro-Creation Practice: Research confirms that beginning with small, completable creative projects significantly builds momentum for larger works by establishing identity as creator rather than mere appreciator.

2. Practice Legacy Project Identification: Studies demonstrate that explicitly framing creative work as potential legacy dramatically enhances motivation and persistence through connection to fundamental meaning needs.

3. Develop Production Scheduling: Psychological research shows that establishing consistent creation periods, however brief, substantially increases completed output by converting sporadic inspiration into sustainable creative practice.

100. Not using my talents or skills to contribute to the world

This regret reflects what vocational psychologists call "talent contribution gap" – the discrepancy between capabilities and their application toward meaningful purposes beyond self-interest. The psychological foundation involves what purpose researchers term "skill compartmentalization" – the artificial separation of abilities from their potential prosocial applications.

This separation creates what meaning theorists identify as "contribution blindness" – failure to recognize how personal capabilities could address others' needs and challenges. Research demonstrates that skill application for others' benefit activates what positive psychologists call "signature strength amplification" – the enhanced satisfaction and efficacy that occurs when using core abilities for purposes transcending self-interest.

The consequences manifest in what career researchers term "purpose achievement mismatch" – the uncomfortable awareness of excellence in areas that feel ultimately insignificant. Studies reveal that individuals who redirect professional-level skills toward prosocial aims report significantly higher levels of meaning, fulfillment, and identity integration compared to those applying similar abilities solely for personal advancement.

Three evidence-based strategies for talent redirection:

1. Implement Skill Inventory Assessment: Research shows that systematically cataloging your capabilities and identifying their potential social applications significantly enhances recognition of contribution opportunities.

2. Practice Professional-Volunteer Skill Alignment: Studies demonstrate that selecting service opportunities utilizing professional-level abilities substantially increases both impact and personal satisfaction compared to generic volunteering.

3. Develop Skill Donation Structures: Psychological research confirms that establishing regular periods for applying expertise to prosocial aims dramatically increases follow-through on contribution intentions through environmental pre-commitment.

101. Not being the role model I wanted to be for my children or others

This regret exemplifies what social learning theorists call "modeling inconsistency" – the disconnect between values verbally endorsed and behaviors actually demonstrated. The psychological mechanism involves what cognitive scientists term "moral licensing" – the tendency to justify contradicting one's stated values through prior or intended virtuous actions.

This licensing creates what integrity researchers identify as "value-behavior incongruence" – living in ways that contradict explicitly held principles. Research demonstrates that congruent modeling affects others through what neuroscientists call "mirror neuron activation" – the automatic neural simulation of observed behaviors that facilitates their adoption, making demonstrated values far more influential than merely stated ones.

The consequences extend beyond influence efficacy to identity coherence. Studies reveal that individuals with greater consistency between professed values and actual behavior report significantly higher levels of self-respect, reduced internal conflict, and enhanced wellbeing compared to those exhibiting substantial discrepancies – producing what integrity researchers term "congruence satisfaction" central to authentic living.

Three evidence-based strategies for congruent modeling:

1. Implement Value Priority Clarification: Research confirms that explicitly identifying your most essential values substantially enhances behavioral alignment by reducing competing priorities that often create inconsistency.

2. Practice Public Accountability: Studies demonstrate that sharing value commitments with others significantly increases follow-through due to enhanced self-awareness and social reinforcement that supports integrity.

3. Develop Behavioral Congruence Reflection: Psychological research shows that regularly examining alignment between actions and values dramatically reduces unconscious hypocrisy through heightened awareness of potential disconnects.

102. Focusing on trivial or selfish pursuits instead of helping people

This regret reflects what meaning researchers call "significance orientation deficit" – directing life energy toward activities lacking meaningful impact despite the psychological benefits of contribution. The psychological foundation involves what behavioral economists term "hedonic focus" – prioritizing immediate pleasure or distraction over activities with deeper but less immediate satisfaction.

This focus creates what purpose theorists identify as "meaning malnourishment" – the gradual diminishment of fulfillment that occurs when life lacks contribution to purposes beyond self-interest. Research demonstrates that prosocial engagement activates what positive psychologists call "eudaimonic wellbeing" – satisfaction derived from living virtuously rather than merely pleasantly, which provides more sustainable happiness than purely hedonic pursuits.

The consequences manifest in what developmental psychologists term "generativity stagnation" – the uncomfortable sense of inconsequentiality that emerges when life impact remains limited to personal concerns. Studies reveal that individuals who regularly engage in helping behaviors report significantly higher levels of meaning, life satisfaction, and reduced depression compared to those primarily focused on personal enjoyment or accumulation.

Three evidence-based strategies for significance reorientation:

1. Implement Time Allocation Analysis: Research shows that periodically examining how you invest time substantially enhances alignment with deeper values by revealing potential discrepancies between stated priorities and actual behavior.
2. Practice Hedonic-Eudaimonic Integration: Studies demonstrate that deliberately selecting activities providing both personal enjoyment and meaningful contribution significantly increases sustainability compared to attempted self-sacrifice.
3. Develop Impact Awareness: Psychological research confirms that regularly reflecting on how your actions affect others dramatically enhances motivation for prosocial behavior by increasing salience of contribution opportunities.

103. Staying silent when I should have spoken up for what was right

This regret exemplifies what moral psychologists call "ethical inaction syndrome" – the failure to voice opposition to wrongdoing despite personal recognition of its impropriety. The psychological mechanism involves what social scientists term "diffusion of responsibility" – the diminished sense of personal obligation to intervene when others are also witnessing problematic situations.

This diffusion creates what integrity researchers identify as "moral self-discrepancy" – the uncomfortable gap between one's ethical self-concept and actual behavior in challenging situations. Research demonstrates that moral courage activates what neuroscientists call "value-congruent processing" – neural activation patterns associated with authenticity and self-respect that enhance psychological well-being beyond the specific ethical situation.

The consequences extend beyond individual integrity to collective ethics. Studies reveal that ethical voice behavior significantly influences group norms through what organizational psychologists call "moral contagion" – the amplification of ethical standards when individuals demonstrate courage during challenging situations. This influence creates what social scientists term "ethical ripple effects" that extend far beyond the original incident.

Three evidence-based strategies for ethical voice development:

1. Implement Values Clarification Exercise: Research shows that explicitly identifying core personal values significantly enhances moral courage by providing clear internal standards against which to evaluate situations requiring potential intervention.
2. Practice Moral Scenario Rehearsal: Studies demonstrate that mentally preparing responses to potential ethical challenges substantially increases appropriate action when similar situations arise through reduced decision complexity during emotional activation.
3. Develop Courage Community: Psychological research confirms that cultivating relationships with similarly values-oriented individuals dramatically enhances moral courage through both accountability and support during challenging ethical situations.

104. Not standing up against injustice or wrongdoing when I witnessed it

This regret reflects what justice researchers call "bystander paralysis" – remaining inactive during witnessed wrongdoing despite personal capability to intervene. The psychological foundation involves what social psychologists term "pluralistic ignorance" – interpreting others' inaction as evidence that intervention is unnecessary or inappropriate, creating collective passivity despite individual concern.

This interpretation creates what moral psychologists identify as "responsibility diffusion" – the dilution of personal obligation across multiple witnesses that reduces individual intervention likelihood. Research demonstrates that active intervention fulfills what developmental theorists call "moral agency needs" – the psychological requirement to express core values through behavior that affects meaningful outcomes.

The consequences manifest in what integrity researchers term "moral identity atrophy" – the gradual weakening of ethical self-concept that occurs when one repeatedly fails to act according to core values. Studies reveal that individuals who intervene against injustice report significantly higher levels of self-respect, meaning, and reduced regret compared to those who remain passive despite similar value systems.

Three evidence-based strategies for intervention capacity:

1. Implement Precommitment Strategy: Research confirms that establishing specific intervention intentions for potential situations significantly increases appropriate action by removing in-the-moment deliberation during emotionally charged events.
2. Practice Micro-Courage Behaviors: Studies demonstrate that deliberately engaging in small acts of moral courage substantially builds capacity for larger interventions through gradual expansion of ethical action comfort zones.
3. Develop Intervention Skill Building: Psychological research shows that acquiring specific techniques for effective intervention dramatically enhances both willingness and effectiveness in addressing wrongdoing through increased response confidence.

105. Never having children (and missing the experience of parenthood and family legacy)

This regret exemplifies what developmental psychologists call "generativity pathway absence" – the unrealized potential for nurturing and guiding the next generation through parenthood. The psychological mechanism involves what decision theorists term "reversible choice illusion" – the misperception that parenthood decisions can be indefinitely postponed despite fertility's biological constraints.

This illusion creates what life-course researchers identify as "developmental foreclosure" – the permanent closure of significant life experiences that can occur without conscious decision through passive postponement. Research demonstrates that parenthood provides what attachment theorists call "generative fulfillment" – satisfaction of the fundamental human need to contribute to the continuation and welfare of subsequent generations.

The consequences extend beyond missed experience to identity formation. Studies reveal that childlessness regret stems not merely from social expectation but often from what meaning researchers call "biographical incompleteness" – the subjective sense that a significant life chapter remains unwritten. This incompleteness produces what developmental psychologists term "generativity crisis" – the struggle to find alternative channels for nurturing and legacy when biological parenthood is no longer possible.

Three evidence-based strategies for generativity development:

1. Implement Alternative Nurturing Pathways: Research shows that actively engaging in mentoring, teaching, or other forms of contributing to younger generations significantly fulfills generative needs even without biological parenthood.
2. Practice Conscious Childlessness Processing: Studies demonstrate that deliberately exploring and acknowledging feelings about not having children substantially enhances psychological integration and reduces unresolved regret.
3. Develop Legacy Alternatives: Psychological research confirms that creating enduring contributions through creative works, community impact, or relationship investment provides meaningful generativity expression that addresses legacy concerns beyond genetic continuity.

106. Failing to invest in or support the younger generation (whether my own family or others)

This regret reflects what developmental psychologists call "generativity neglect" – insufficient investment in nurturing the next generation despite its importance for both societal continuation and personal fulfillment. The psychological foundation involves what attention researchers term "temporal myopia" – focusing on immediate concerns at the expense of long-term relational investments with profound delayed benefits.

This myopia creates what generativity theorists identify as "nurturing opportunity blindness" – failure to recognize chances to positively influence younger individuals' development. Research demonstrates that intergenerational investment fulfills what Erik Erikson termed the "generativity versus stagnation" developmental task essential for psychological well-being in middle and later adulthood.

The consequences manifest in what meaning researchers call "impact limitation" – the restricted sphere of positive influence that results from neglecting younger generation engagement. Studies reveal that individuals who actively mentor and support youth report significantly higher levels of purpose, meaning, and legacy satisfaction compared to those with similar capacities who don't engage in such investment.

Three evidence-based strategies for generational investment:

1. Implement Generativity Mapping: Research confirms that systematically identifying your specific knowledge, skills, and wisdom that could benefit younger individuals significantly enhances recognition of meaningful investment opportunities.
2. Practice Structured Mentoring Engagement: Studies demonstrate that establishing regular, purposeful interaction with younger individuals substantially increases both impact and personal satisfaction through consistent rather than sporadic investment.
3. Develop Intergenerational Bridge Building: Psychological research shows that creating deliberate connections between your generation's experiences and current youth challenges dramatically enhances relevant wisdom transmission and relationship quality.

107. Realizing too late that personal success meant little without making an impact on others

This regret exemplifies what meaning researchers call "achievement-significance disparity" – the recognition that accomplishments lacking positive impact on others ultimately provide limited fulfillment. The psychological mechanism involves what motivational scientists term "extrinsic goal dominance" – organizing life around external markers of success rather than intrinsic values that typically include contribution.

This dominance creates what purpose researchers identify as "success hollowness" – the sense of emptiness that often accompanies achievement lacking meaningful positive impact on others. Research demonstrates that contribution functions as what positive psychologists call a "hedonic amplifier" – enhancing satisfaction from accomplishments when they benefit others beyond oneself through what we term "self-transcendent purpose."

The consequences extend beyond retrospective evaluation to present well-being. Studies reveal that individuals whose success benefits others report significantly higher levels of meaning, life satisfaction, and reduced depression compared to those with similar achievements lacking prosocial impact. This advantage stems from what purpose theorists call "psychological mattering" – the sense that one's existence makes a positive difference in the world.

Three evidence-based strategies for impact integration:

1. Implement Success-Impact Alignment: Research shows that deliberately identifying how your strengths and accomplishments could benefit others significantly enhances fulfillment through connecting personal success with meaningful contribution.
2. Practice Legacy Perspective Taking: Studies demonstrate that periodically evaluating decisions from the viewpoint of your future legacy substantially improves choices by highlighting impact considerations alongside achievement metrics.
3. Develop Contribution Retrofitting: Psychological research confirms that identifying ways existing skills and resources can be redirected toward prosocial impact dramatically enhances meaning even late in life by connecting past accomplishments with present contribution.

108. Not preserving my family's stories or history for future generations

This regret reflects what cultural psychologists call "narrative heritage loss" – the disappearance of family history and wisdom that occurs when stories remain undocumented. The psychological foundation involves what temporal researchers term "intergenerational communication postponement" – the consistent delay of family history sharing until advanced age when cognitive or physical limitations often impair transmission.

This postponement creates what identity theorists identify as "narrative continuity disruption" – the broken chain of family stories that provide crucial context for understanding both personal and collective origins. Research demonstrates that family narratives serve as what developmental psychologists call "identity anchors" – stories that connect individuals to something larger than themselves, providing meaning and psychological grounding.

The consequences extend beyond lost information to psychological functioning. Studies reveal that individuals with greater knowledge of family history demonstrate enhanced resilience, stronger identity formation, and superior coping skills compared to those lacking such narrative connections – producing what researchers term "intergenerational resilience transmission" through shared stories rather than genetics alone.

Three evidence-based strategies for heritage preservation:

1. Implement Story Capture System: Research confirms that establishing simple, consistent methods for recording family stories (audio recordings, journals, photo documentation) dramatically increases preservation compared to relying on memory transmission alone.
2. Practice Intergenerational Story Sessions: Studies demonstrate that creating structured opportunities for older family members to share experiences with younger generations substantially enhances both transmission quality and relationship depth.
3. Develop Heritage Curation Habits: Psychological research shows that regularly organizing and contextualizing family artifacts and stories creates accessible heritage resources that significantly strengthen family identity across generations.

109. Not being remembered as a good person due to my actions

This regret exemplifies what legacy researchers call "reputation-character incongruence" – the distressing awareness that one's remembered identity may reflect unfavorable rather than aspirational qualities. The psychological mechanism involves what behavioral scientists term "immediate-impact blindness" – underestimating how specific actions affect others' perceptions despite their cumulative importance for reputation.

This blindness creates what identity theorists identify as "narrative contamination" – the presence of actions that undermine positive life stories others construct about us after death. Research demonstrates that reputation concerns reflect what terror management theorists call "symbolic immortality striving" – the desire to be remembered positively as a buffer against mortality anxiety and a form of existence beyond physical death.

The consequences manifest in what integrity researchers term "biographical coherence threat" – the uncomfortable awareness that one's life story lacks the ethical consistency that underlies positive remembrance. Studies reveal that individuals who align behavior with aspirational values report significantly greater peace with mortality and reduced end-of-life distress compared to those recognizing substantial discrepancies between ideal and actual behavior.

Three evidence-based strategies for legacy alignment:

1. Implement Reputation Reflection Exercise: Research shows that periodically considering how specific behaviors might be remembered significantly enhances decision quality by highlighting character implications that immediate concerns often obscure.
2. Practice Virtue Consistency Audit: Studies demonstrate that regularly examining alignment between core values and actual behavior substantially improves ethical consistency through increased awareness of potential disconnects.
3. Develop Relationship Repair Priorities: Psychological research confirms that identifying and addressing past relational harms dramatically enhances how one is remembered by transforming damaged relationships into potential sources of positive legacy.

110. Not thanking or acknowledging the people who helped me along my journey

This regret reflects what gratitude researchers call "appreciation expression deficit" – the failure to communicate genuine thankfulness to those who provided significant support despite its relational importance. The psychological foundation involves what cognitive scientists term "contribution invisibility" – the tendency to underrecognize how others' actions facilitated our achievements through what social psychologists call the "self-serving bias."

This invisibility creates what relationship researchers identify as "gratitude gap" – the discrepancy between felt and expressed appreciation that diminishes connection quality. Research demonstrates that gratitude expression activates what positive psychologists call "positive relationship spirals" – mutual cycles of appreciation and support that strengthen bonds through reciprocal positive reinforcement.

The consequences extend beyond relationship quality to well-being. Studies reveal that individuals who regularly express gratitude demonstrate enhanced immune function, reduced blood pressure, improved sleep quality, and greater relationship satisfaction compared to those who experience but don't express similar levels of thankfulness – creating what health psychologists term "embodied appreciation benefits" for both recipients and expressers.

Three evidence-based strategies for gratitude expression:

1. Implement Contribution Inventory: Research confirms that systematically identifying individuals who significantly impacted your life journey dramatically increases appropriate acknowledgment by making contributions consciously visible.

2. Practice Specific Gratitude Communication: Studies demonstrate that expressing appreciation with detailed recognition of particular contributions substantially enhances impact compared to general thanks through deeper validation of the helper's specific efforts.

3. Develop Gratitude Completion Project: Psychological research shows that deliberately creating a plan to thank previously unacknowledged contributors creates meaningful closure and relationship enhancement even when considerable time has passed.

111. Not doing my part to leave the world a better place (for example, not protecting the environment or helping my community more)

This regret exemplifies what environmental psychologists call "stewardship deficit syndrome" – insufficient care for collective welfare despite its importance for both societal sustainability and personal meaning. The psychological mechanism involves what behavioral economists term "commons dilemma" – the tendency to prioritize individual benefit over collective good despite the latter's ultimate necessity for individual flourishing.

This prioritization creates what sustainability researchers identify as "future impact blindness" – underappreciation of how current actions affect subsequent generations and broader ecosystems. Research demonstrates that environmental and community contribution fulfills what purpose theorists call "transcendent meaning needs" – the psychological requirement to contribute to something larger and more enduring than individual existence.

The consequences manifest in what meaning researchers term "contribution vacuum" – the sense of having taken from collective resources without adequate reciprocal investment. Studies reveal that individuals engaged in community and environmental stewardship report significantly higher levels of life satisfaction, meaning, and reduced death anxiety compared to those focused primarily on personal concerns – producing what positive psychologists call "sustainable well-being" that benefits both individual and collective welfare.

Three evidence-based strategies for stewardship development:

1. Implement Impact Sphere Identification: Research shows that identifying specific domains where your particular skills and resources could meaningfully contribute significantly enhances effective stewardship through targeted rather than generic engagement.

2. Practice Legacy Action Planning: Studies demonstrate that deliberately selecting contribution activities with potential multigenerational impact substantially increases both motivation and fulfillment through connection to fundamental meaning needs.

3. Develop Stewardship Integration: Psychological research confirms that embedding contribution within existing routines and interests dramatically increases sustainable engagement compared to approaches requiring separate time and identity commitments.

Chapter 9. How to Live a Life with Fewer Regrets

Translating End-of-Life Wisdom into Present Well-Being

Researchers on human flourishing have discovered few data sources as compelling as the reflections of those nearing life's end. These perspectives offer what might be called "empirical wisdom" – insights distilled through the clarifying lens of mortality that reveal consistent patterns regardless of background, culture, or circumstance.

The regrets we've explored in this book aren't merely cautionary tales; they constitute a remarkable dataset on what humans ultimately find meaningful. By systematically analyzing these patterns, we can derive evidence-based principles for deliberately cultivating a life viewed with satisfaction rather than regret.

Let me offer a framework for translating this wisdom into practical strategies for flourishing:

Relationship Investment as Primary Well-Being Strategy

Research consistently demonstrates that relationship quality predicts life satisfaction more reliably than any other variable, including wealth, achievement, or even physical health. This finding aligns perfectly with what those at life's end repeatedly emphasize: the centrality of human connection.

The practical implications are clear: Make deliberate, consistent investments in meaningful relationships. Express love and appreciation explicitly rather than assuming it's understood. Practice what we call "active-constructive responding" – engaging fully when others share good news or vulnerable feelings. Resolve conflicts promptly, as relationship research clearly shows that conflict itself doesn't predict relationship failure – but the failure to repair does.

Most importantly, recognize that time is the currency of relationships. No amount of material resources can compensate for its absence. As one research participant poignantly noted, "I built a beautiful house that my children rarely visit because I wasn't there when they needed me."

Authentic Living as Psychological Integration

A second consistent pattern in end-of-life reflections involves what psychologists call "self-concordance" – the alignment between behavior and deeply held values. Those who live authentically report significantly less regret than those who pursue paths dictated primarily by external expectations.

This finding suggests a crucial life strategy: Develop clarity about your personal values, then create decision-making frameworks that prioritize these values over social convention or others' expectations. Research demonstrates that even small shifts toward greater authenticity produce substantial increases in well-being and significantly reduce what we call "intrapsychic conflict" – the internal tension created by living incongruently.

This doesn't mean reckless self-indulgence. Rather, it means thoughtfully examining which external expectations genuinely serve your values and which merely divert you from a life of meaning and purpose.

Presence as Experiential Enhancement

A third consistent regret pattern reveals what cognitive scientists call "temporal focus displacement" – the tendency to mentally remove ourselves from present experience through rumination about the past or anxiety about the future. This displacement creates what might be called "experiential thinning" – a diminished engagement with life as it unfolds.

The research-based antidote involves cultivating what we call "psychological presence" – the capacity to fully engage with current experience. Studies demonstrate that even brief mindfulness practices significantly enhance both subjective well-being and the richness of memory formation. By attending fully to experiences as they occur, you essentially live more life within the same chronological period.

This presence extends beyond sensory experience to emotional engagement. Allow yourself to experience joy without guilt, adventure without excessive caution, and playfulness without concern for appearing dignified. Research consistently shows that positive emotions build psychological resources that enhance resilience during inevitable difficult periods.

Work Integration Rather Than Domination

The data from end-of-life reflections reveals a consistent pattern regarding work: it's rarely the hours devoted to meaningful work that people regret, but rather work that dominates to the exclusion of other life dimensions.

This suggests a strategy of what organizational psychologists call "work-life integration" rather than rigid separation. Seek work that aligns with your values and strengths, establish appropriate boundaries, and recognize that professional achievement functions best as one component of well-being rather than its primary source.

The research is clear: those who define success solely through career advancement demonstrate significantly higher regret intensity than those who maintain what we call "life domain balance" – appropriate investment across multiple areas of meaning and importance.

Preventive Health as Freedom Expansion

Health-related regrets feature prominently in end-of-life reflections, yet research reveals a fascinating paradox: health is typically taken for granted until compromised, at which point it dominates consciousness. This pattern creates what health psychologists call "prevention awareness asymmetry" – insufficient motivation for health-protective behaviors despite their crucial importance.

The evidence-based approach involves reconceptualizing health behaviors not as sacrifices but as investments in future freedom and capacity. Regular physical activity, nutritious eating patterns, adequate sleep, and stress management create what we call "capability extension" – the prolongation of physical and cognitive independence that enables pursuit of meaningful goals across the lifespan.

Perhaps most importantly, mental health maintenance deserves equal priority with physical well-being. Research demonstrates that untreated psychological distress significantly compromises quality of life while responding remarkably well to appropriate intervention.

Transcendence Through Contribution

A final consistent pattern in end-of-life reflections involves contribution beyond self-interest. Those who invested in helping others, supporting causes, or creating lasting impact report significantly less regret than those who focused primarily on personal advancement or pleasure.

This finding aligns with what positive psychology identifies as "self-transcendence" – the extension of concern and action beyond individual welfare to encompass broader welfare. Research demonstrates that contribution creates what we call "meaning amplification" – the enhanced sense of purpose and significance that comes from positively affecting others' lives.

The practical implication is clear: Deliberately incorporate contribution into your life design. Whether through parenting, mentoring, community involvement, or broader social impact, transcending self-interest creates a psychological legacy that significantly enhances life satisfaction upon reflection.

Integration: The PERMA Framework Applied to Regret Prevention

These patterns align remarkably well with what research has identified as the five core elements of well-being, which I've termed the PERMA model:

Positive emotion – Cultivating joy, gratitude, serenity, interest, hope, pride, amusement, inspiration, awe, and love **Engagement** – Experiencing flow and complete absorption in meaningful activities **Relationships** – Building and maintaining positive connections with others **Meaning** – Belonging to and serving something larger than oneself **Achievement** – Pursuing mastery, accomplishment, and success

What end-of-life regrets reveal is that these elements aren't merely components of present happiness but predictors of eventual life satisfaction. By deliberately investing in each domain, you're not just enhancing current well-being but constructing a life that will ultimately be viewed with fulfillment rather than regret.

The Psychology of Prospective Living

Perhaps the most transformative insight from regret research is this: we need not wait until life's end to gain perspective on what matters. Through what psychologists call "prospective hindsight" – imagining looking back on current choices from a future vantage point – we can access the clarity that mortality typically provides without requiring its immediacy.

When facing significant decisions, ask yourself: "When I eventually reflect on this choice from life's end, which option will I wish I had selected?" This simple but powerful cognitive strategy activates what we call "the wisdom of projected regret" – using anticipated future perspective to guide present choices.

While no life unfolds without some regrets – indeed, research suggests a complete absence of regret often indicates insufficient risk-taking or growth – deliberate application of these principles can significantly reduce their intensity and prevalence.

The science is clear: love deeply and express it openly; live authentically according to your values; remain present to experience; balance work with other meaningful dimensions; maintain physical and mental health; and contribute beyond yourself. These evidence-based practices don't merely minimize regret – they actively construct what Aristotle called eudaimonia – a life of virtue, meaning, and excellence.

Each day presents another opportunity to align your choices with what ultimately matters. The wisdom distilled from countless lives before you offers a remarkable gift: the chance to benefit from their hindsight while you still have time to shape your path forward.

Chapter 10. Sources and References

The insights and reflections presented in this book are derived from a variety of sources, including academic studies, expert opinions, and real-world testimonials. The following sources were instrumental in compiling the 111 most common regrets people have at the end of life:

- Bronnie Ware's Study on Regrets of the Dying – The Top Five Regrets of the Dying (2011)
- Shai Davidai & Thomas Gilovich (2018) – The Ideal Road Not Taken – Published in Emotion (APA)
- Daniel Kahneman & Amos Tversky – Loss Aversion Theory
- Neal Roese – The Function of Regret (2005)
- Laura Carstensen's Socioemotional Selectivity Theory (1999) – Stanford University
- The Top Five Regrets of the Dying – Bronnie Ware
- If Only: How to Turn Regret Into Opportunity – Neal Roese
- The Power of Regret: How Looking Backward Moves Us Forward – Daniel Pink
- Being Mortal: Medicine and What Matters in the End – Atul Gawande
- Studies on end-of-life reflections and what older adults regret the most
- Research on career regrets published by Harvard Business Review and Forbes
- Work by Barry Schwartz on the Paradox of Choice
- Interviews with hospice care workers, nurses, and doctors
- Online discussions from Reddit threads, social media, and public forums
- Insights from therapists, life coaches, and counselors
- Cross-cultural studies on deathbed reflections
- Religious and philosophical texts on regret, life fulfillment, and purpose
- Longitudinal studies like the Harvard Study of Adult Development